Activities Manual / Study Guide
to accompany

Looking Out / Looking In
EIGHTH EDITION

Ronald B. Adler
Neil Towne

Prepared by
Mary O. Wiemann
Santa Barbara City College

Harcourt Brace College Publishers

Fort Worth Philadelphia San Diego New York Orlando Austin San Antonio
Toronto Montreal London Sydney Tokyo

Address editorial correspondence to:
Harcourt Brace College Publishers
301 Commerce Street, Suite 3700
Fort Worth, Texas 76102

Address Orders To:
Harcourt Brace & Company
Permissions Department
6277 Sea Harbor Drive
Orlando, Florida 32887-6777
1-800-782-4479 or 1-800-433-0001 (in Florida)

Printed in the United States of America

6 7 8 9 0 1 2 3 4   066   10 9 8 7 6 5 4 3 2

C O N T E N T S

CHAPTER 5   LANGUAGE: BARRIER AND BRIDGE

CHAPTER 6   NONVERBAL COMMUNICATION: MESSAGES WITHOUT WORDS

CHAPTER 9 IMPROVING COMMUNICATION CLIMATES

CHAPTER 10 MANAGING INTERPERSONAL CONFLICTS

PREFACE

Welcome to the new Activities Manual /Study Guide for *Looking Out/Looking In*, Eighth Edition. Responding to feedback from Activities Manual users around the country, this Activities Manual/Study Guide presents a new format for student learning. The best and most-used activities from the past editions have been retained, and a new and extensive study guide has been added. Thus, this edition of the Activities Manual/Study Guide contains more than 50 class-tested exercises and more than 500 study test items designed to build understanding of principles and proficiency in skills introduced in the text.

Each chapter in the Activities Manual/Study Guide parallels the chapter in *Looking Out/Looking In*. The following areas in each chapter combine to provide a thorough, student-centered learning package:

•**Outlines**   Extended outlines of each chapter begin each section. Many instructors ask students to use the outlines as a lecture guide in class or a place to take notes as they read the chapter.

•**Key Terms**   Vocabulary terms for each chapter follow the outlines; they are spaced so that students can write in definitions for each term in the Study Guide. This helps students study for exams and focus on important concepts.

•**Activities**   Students who complete the activities in this manual will develop understanding and skill in each area through a choice of exercises. Exercises are coded with icons to help you choose how to use them. ❖ denotes a group activity. ◆ identifies an individual one.

> *Skill Builder* activities—designed primarily to help students identify the target behavior in a number of common interpersonal communication situations. These are frequently group activities that reinforce learning in the classroom. They can be done as individual activities.

> *Invitation to Insight* activities—designed to help students discover how newly learned principles can be applied in their everyday lives. They can be grouped together to form a "Communication Journal" for the entire course. While these activities are usually designed for individual use, they can provide the structure for small group discussion or lecture/discussion.

> *Oral Skill* activities—designed to allow students to actually exhibit communication behaviors they have studied. They are designed for individual, dyadic, or small group use in a classroom or lab setting.

Many of the activities can be used in a variety of ways. Instructors can adapt them, use some or all, grade them or leave them ungraded, assign them as out-of-class exercises, or use them as class enrichment. Student observations in many exercises will lead to class discussions on how to apply the newly learned principles in the "real world" of one's interpersonal relationships.

While they almost always stimulate class discussion, the activities in this manual are designed to do more than keep a class busy or interested. If they are used regularly, they will help students to move beyond simply understanding the principles of interpersonal communication and actually to perform more effectively in a variety of communication situations.

Study Guide activities—designed to help students identify major concepts or skills contained in the chapter. They are designed to be done individually, in groups, or with the entire class, and they have answer keys found at the end of each chapter. Matching, True/False, Completion, and Multiple Choice items review and reinforce for students as they work at their own pace.

The new Activities Manual/Study Guide should help develop more effective communication.

Mary Wiemann

❖ A First Look at Interpersonal Relationships ❖

OUTLINE

Use this outline to take notes as you read the chapter in the text and/or as your instructor lectures in class.

I. **INTRODUCTION TO INTERPERSONAL COMMUNICATION**
   A. **Communication Is Important**
   B. **We Communicate to Satisfy Needs**
      1. Physical needs
      2. Identity needs
      3. Social needs (Rubin)
         a. Pleasure
         b. Affection
         c. Inclusion
         d. Escape
         e. Relaxation
         f. Control
      4. Practical goals
         a. Instrumental goals
         b. Maslow's basic needs
            1) Physical
            2) Safety
            3) Social
            4) Self-esteem
            5) Self-actualization

II. **THE PROCESS OF COMMUNICATION**
   A. **A Linear View**
      1. Sender
      2. Encoding
      3. Message
      4. Channel
      5. Decoding
      6. Receiver

7. Noise
   a. External (physical)
   b. Physiological
   c. Psychological

B. **An Interactive View**
   1. Feedback
   2. Environments
   3. Static activity

C. **A Transactional View**
   1. Send/receive messages simultaneously
   2. Nonisolated "acts"
   3. Communication is *with* others, not *to* them
   4. Mutual influence

III. **COMMUNICATION PRINCIPLES AND MISCONCEPTIONS**
   A. **Communication Principles**
      1. Communication can be intentional or unintentional
      2. It's impossible not to communicate
      3. Communication is irreversible
      4. Communication is unrepeatable

   B. **Avoiding Communication Misconceptions**
      1. Meanings are not in words
      2. More communication is not always better
      3. Communication will not solve all problems
      4. Communication is not a natural ability

IV. **THE NATURE OF INTERPERSONAL COMMUNICATION**
   A. **Two Views of Interpersonal Communication**
      1. Contextual—dyadic
      2. Qualitative
         a. Uniqueness
         b. Irreplaceability
         c. Interdependence
         d. Disclosure
         e. Intrinsic rewards
         f. Scarcity

   B. **Personal and Impersonal Communication: A Matter of Balance**

V. **COMMUNICATING ABOUT RELATIONSHIPS**
   A. **Content and Relational Messages**

   B. **Metacommunication**

   C. **Types of Relational Messages**
      1. Affinity
      2. Respect

Harcourt Brace & Company

3. Control
    a. Types
        (1) Decisional
        (2) Conversational
    b. Distribution
        (1) Complementary
        (2) Symmetrical
            a) competitive symmetry
            b) submissive symmetry
            c) neutralized symmetry
        (3) Parallel

VI. **COMMUNICATION COMPETENCE: WHAT MAKES AN EFFECTIVE COMMUNICATOR?**

A. **Communication Competence Defined**
    1. No "ideal" way to communicate
    2. Competence is situational
    3. Competence has a relational dimension

B. **Competence Requires Juggling Conflict Goals (Dialectical Tensions)**
    1. Approval versus personal affectiveness
    2. Intimacy versus distance
    3. Autonomy versus connection
    4. Short- versus long-term objectives
    5. Conflicting needs in different relationships

C. **Characteristics of Competent Communicators**
    1. A wide range of behaviors
    2. The ability to choose the most appropriate behavior
        a. Context
        b. Your goal
        c. The other person
    3. Skill at performing behaviors
        a. Beginning awareness
        b. Awkwardness
        c. Skillfulness
        d. Integration
        e. Empathy/perspective-taking
        f. Cognitive complexity
        g. Self-monitoring
    4. Commitment to the relationship
        a. Commitment to the other person
        b. Commitment to the message
        c. A desire for mutual benefit
        d. A desire to interact and to continue the relationship

Harcourt Brace & Company

KEY TERMS

Use these key terms to review major concepts from your text. Write the definition for each key term in the space to the right

affection _____

affinity _____

awareness _____

awkwardness _____

channel _____

cognitive complexity _____

commitment _____

communication _____

communication competence _____

communication misconceptions _____

communication model _____

communication principles _____

competitive symmetry _____

complementary relationship _____

content message _____

context _____

control _____

conversational control _____

decision control _____

decoding _____

dialectical tensions _____

dyad _____

Harcourt Brace & Company

dyadic communication _____

encoding _____

environment _____

escape _____

external noise _____

feedback _____

impersonal communication _____

inclusion _____

influence _____

instrumental goals _____

integration _____

interactive communication model _____

interpersonal communication (contextual and qualitative) _____

interpersonal relationship _____

intimacy _____

linear communication model _____

message _____

metacommunication _____

needs (physical, identity, social) _____

neutralized symmetry _____

noise (external, physiological, psychological) _____

parallel relationship _____

physiological noise _____

pleasure _____

practical goals _____

Harcourt Brace & Company

psychological noise _____

receiver _____

relational message _____

relaxation _____

respect _____

self-actualization _____

self-monitoring _____

sender _____

skillfulness _____

submissive symmetry _____

symmetrical relationship _____

transactional communication model _____

Harcourt Brace & Company

ACTIVITIES

❖ 1.1 COMMUNICATION SKILLS INVENTORY ❖

◆ **Activity Type: Invitation to Insight**

PURPOSES

1. To help you discover how satisfied you are with the way you communicate in various situations.
2. To preview some topics that will be covered in *Looking Out/Looking In*.

INSTRUCTIONS

1. Below you will find several communication-related situations. As you read each item, imagine yourself in that situation.
2. For each instance, answer the following question: *How satisfied am I with the way I would behave in this situation and ones like it?* You can express your answers by placing one of the following numbers in the space by each item:

5 = Completely satisfied with my probable action
4 = Generally, though not totally, satisfied with my probable action
3 = About equally satisfied and dissatisfied with my probable action
2 = Generally, though not totally, dissatisfied with my probable action
1 = Totally dissatisfied with my probable action

_____ 1. A new acquaintance has just shared some personal experiences with you that make you think you'd like to develop a closer relationship. You have experienced the same things and are now deciding whether to reveal these personal experiences. (8)

_____ 2. You've become involved in a political discussion with someone whose views are the complete opposite of yours. The other person asks, "Can't you at least understand why I feel as I do?" (3, 7)

_____ 3. You are considered a responsible adult by virtually everyone except one relative who still wants to help you make all your decisions. You value your relationship with this person, but you need to be seen as more independent. You know you should do something about this situation. (9, 10)

_____ 4. In a mood of self-improvement a friend asks you to describe the one or two ways by which you think he or she could behave better. You're willing to do so, but need to express yourself in a clear and helpful way. (3, 5, 10)

_____ 5. A close companion says that you've been behaving "differently" lately and asks if you know what he or she means. (5, 6, 7)

_____ 6. You've grown to appreciate a new friend a great deal lately, and you realize that you ought to share your feelings. (4)

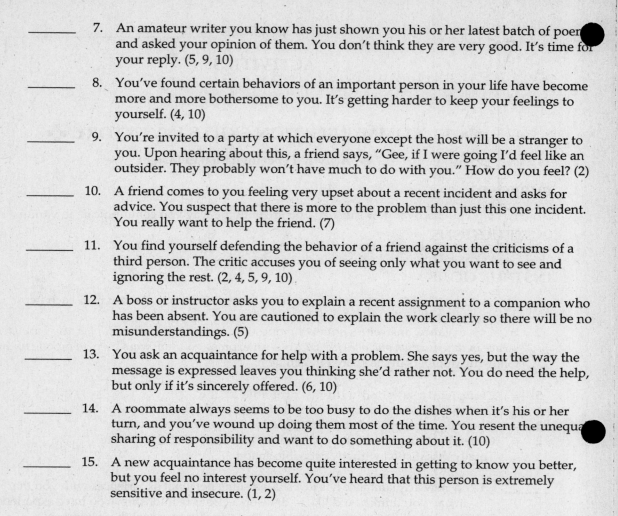

_____ 7. An amateur writer you know has just shown you his or her latest batch of poems and asked your opinion of them. You don't think they are very good. It's time for your reply. (5, 9, 10)

_____ 8. You've found certain behaviors of an important person in your life have become more and more bothersome to you. It's getting harder to keep your feelings to yourself. (4, 10)

_____ 9. You're invited to a party at which everyone except the host will be a stranger to you. Upon hearing about this, a friend says, "Gee, if I were going I'd feel like an outsider. They probably won't have much to do with you." How do you feel? (2)

_____ 10. A friend comes to you feeling very upset about a recent incident and asks for advice. You suspect that there is more to the problem than just this one incident. You really want to help the friend. (7)

_____ 11. You find yourself defending the behavior of a friend against the criticisms of a third person. The critic accuses you of seeing only what you want to see and ignoring the rest. (2, 4, 5, 9, 10)

_____ 12. A boss or instructor asks you to explain a recent assignment to a companion who has been absent. You are cautioned to explain the work clearly so there will be no misunderstandings. (5)

_____ 13. You ask an acquaintance for help with a problem. She says yes, but the way the message is expressed leaves you thinking she'd rather not. You do need the help, but only if it's sincerely offered. (6, 10)

_____ 14. A roommate always seems to be too busy to do the dishes when it's his or her turn, and you've wound up doing them most of the time. You resent the unequal sharing of responsibility and want to do something about it. (10)

_____ 15. A new acquaintance has become quite interested in getting to know you better, but you feel no interest yourself. You've heard that this person is extremely sensitive and insecure. (1, 2)

You can use the results of this survey in two ways. By looking at each question you can see how satisfied you are with your behavior in that specific type of situation. A response of 1 or 2 on any single question is an obvious signal that you can profit from working on that situation. Parenthetical numbers following each item indicate the chapters of _Looking Out/Looking In_ which focus on that subject.

By totaling your score for all of the items you can get an idea of how satisfied you are with your overall ability to communicate in interpersonal situations. A score of 68–75 suggests high satisfaction, 58–67 indicates moderate satisfaction, while 45–57 shows that you feel dissatisfied with your communication behavior nearly half the time.

Another valuable way to use this activity is to make a second inventory at the end of the course. Have you improved? Are there still areas you will need to work on?

Harcourt Brace & Company

✚ 1.2 EXPANDING YOUR COMMUNICATION EFFECTIVENESS ✚

◆ Activity Type: Invitation to Insight

PURPOSES

1. To help you broaden your repertoire of effective communication behaviors and your skill at performing them.
2. To help you identify the most appropriate communication behaviors in important situations.

INSTRUCTIONS

1. Use the space below to identify two areas in which you would like to communicate more effectively.
2. For each area, identify a person you have observed who communicates in a way that you think would improve your effectiveness. Describe this person's communication behavior.
3. Describe how you could adapt these behaviors to your own life.

EXAMPLE

a. Area in which you would like to communicate more effectively
    Making conversation with people I've just met.
b. Model who communicates effectively in this area *My friend Rich*
c. Model's behavior *He asks sincere questions of people he's just met, compliments them enthusiastically, and smiles a lot.*
d. How could you apply these behaviors? *I can spend more time thinking about people I've just met and less time thinking self-consciously about my own nervousness. Then I can focus on parts of these new people that interest me and let the other person know I'm interested. The key seems to be sincerity: I have to really mean what I say and not use questions and compliments as tricks.*

SITUATION 1

a. Area in which you would like to communicate more effectively

    _____

b. Model who communicates effectively in this area _____

c. Model's behavior _____

    _____

d. How could you apply these behaviors? _____

    _____

    _____

SITUATION 2

    a. Area in which you would like to communicate more effectively

        _____

    b. Model who communicates effectively in this area _____

    c. Model's behavior _____

        _____

    d. How could you apply these behaviors? _____

        _____

        _____

        _____

SITUATION 3

    a. Area in which you would like to communicate more effectively

        _____

    b. Model who communicates effectively in this area _____

    c. Model's behavior _____

        _____

    d. How could you apply these behaviors? _____

        _____

        _____

        _____

Harcourt Brace & Company

❖ 1.3 RECOGNIZING RELATIONAL MESSAGES ❖

◆❖ Activity Type: Skill Builder

PURPOSES

1. To illustrate that virtually every message has both a content and a relational dimension.
2. To give you practice recognizing the relational dimension of common messages.
3. To demonstrate that relational messages are ambiguous and need to be verified by perception-checking statements.

INSTRUCTIONS

1. Describe the relational issues that seem to be involved in each of the situations listed below.
2. Record examples of your own messages and identify the relational levels involved.

Content Level	Relational Level (Inclusion, Control, Affection, Respect)
Example: *Students and instructor disagree about whether testing and grading system is fair.*	**Control:** *Students' right to help shape courses.* **Respect:** *Whether instructor values opinions of students.*
1. A friend asks if you want to come over and share a bottle of wine.	
2. Wife complains that husband doesn't help out enough around the house.	
3. Boss asks your opinion about making changes in business.	
4. Couple argues about whose family to visit over holidays.	
5. Friend A teases friend B in good-natured way about B's bad memory.	
6. Employees object to management's requirement that all illnesses be verified by a doctor's note.	
7. Several old acquaintances call to ask if you'll be attending a high school reunion.	

Harcourt Brace & Company

Content Level	Relational Level (Inclusion, Control, Affection, Respect)
8. Roommate sighs, grimaces, and says, "all right" when you ask for a ride.	
9. Parents remind teenager to drive carefully every time he or she goes out.	
10. Doctor's receptionist puts you on hold for five minutes when you call to make an appointment.	
11. Roommate nods, smiles and says, "Sure, that's a great idea."	
12. Student asks the professor, "Can you suggest any more books on that subject?"	
13. Family member says to college student, "You have to come home for the holidays! Everybody wants to see you!"	
14. "We really must get together sometime," a co-worker says with enthusiasm.	
15. "I know you're trying hard," a fellow student says flatly, looking away from you.	
Now, record examples of messages you've sent or that were sent to you (content)—and identify the relational dimension(s) of the message.	
16.	
17.	
18.	

Harcourt Brace & Company

❖ 1.4 COMMUNICATION COMPETENCE ❖

❖ Activity Type: Skill Builder

PURPOSES

1. To examine a relationship that functions effectively.
2. To present the aspects of competence at work in the relationship.
3. To compare competent relationships.

INSTRUCTIONS

1. Form groups to get to know one another.
2. Describe an important relationship in which you are involved to the other group members.
3. Describe the aspects of communication competence that are/are not at work in this relationship (range of behaviors, ability to choose the most appropriate behavior, skill at performing behavior, ability to view issues from a variety of perspectives, ability to monitor behavior while communicating, and commitment to the relationship)
4. Comment on your satisfaction with the relationship, and the role you play in that satisfaction.
5. Respond to other group members as they describe their relationships.

RELATIONSHIP: _____

Aspects of communication competence:

Range of behaviors _____

Ability to choose appropriate behaviors _____

Skill at performing behavior _____

Ability to view issues from a variety of perspectives _____

Ability to monitor behavor _____

Commitment to the relationship _____

Satisfaction with relationship _____

Role you play in the relationship _____

Responses to others' relationships _____

Harcourt Brace & Company

STUDY GUIDE

CHECK YOUR UNDERSTANDING

MATCHING (KEY TERM REVIEW)

_____ 1. dialectical tensions

_____ 2. noise

_____ 3. affection

_____ 4. channel

_____ 5. affinity

_____ 6. cognitive complexity

_____ 7. communication competence

_____ 8. environment

_____ 9. dyad

_____ 10. encoding

_____ 11. feedback

_____ 12. inclusion

_____ 13. interpersonal communication

_____ 14. decoding

_____ 15. control

_____ 16. impersonal communication

_____ 17. content message

_____ 18. relational message

_____ 19. sender

_____ 20. receiver

a. any force that interferes with effective communication

b. the degree to which persons like or appreciate one another

c. the ability to construct a variety of frameworks for viewing an issue

d. goal conflicts that arise when two opposing or incompatible forces exist simultaneously

e. the medium through which a message passes from sender to receiver

f. the ability to accomplish one's personal goals in a manner that maintains a relationship on terms that are acceptable to all parties

g. the social need to care for others and to be cared for by them

h. the process of putting thoughts into symbols, most commonly words

i. the field of experiences that leads a person to make sense of another's behavior

j. two individuals communicating

k. the social need to influence others

l. the process in which a receiver attaches meaning to a message

m. behavior that treats others as objects rather than individuals

n. the social need to feel a sense of belonging in some relationship with others

o. the creator of a message

p. the discernible response of a receiver to a sender's message

q. communication in which the parties consider one another as unique individuals rather than as objects

r. a message that expresses the social relationship between two or more individuals

s. one who notices and attends to a message

t. a message that communicates information about the subject being discussed

Harcourt Brace & Company

TRUE/FALSE

Mark the statements below as true or false. Correct statements that are false on the lines below to create a true statement.

_____ 1. Studies show your physical health may be affected by communication.

_____

_____

_____ 2. People with high self-esteem are confident in themselves, so they are more likely to seek out people who treat them poorly as a test of their confidence.

_____

_____

_____ 3. Communication skills are more important in helping you get a job than in keeping the job or performing it well.

_____

_____

_____ 4. Instrumental goals are the same thing as social needs.

_____

_____

_____ 5. Psychologist Abraham Maslow claims that basic needs must be satisfied before people concern themselves with higher order needs.

_____

_____

_____ 6. The interactive view of communication suggests that communication flows in one direction, from sender to receiver.

_____

_____

Harcourt Brace & Company

_____ 7. The transactional model of communication shows that communication is something we do *to* others.

_____

_____

_____ 8. It's impossible not to communicate.

_____

_____

_____ 9. Luckily, communication will always help us solve our problems.

_____

_____

_____ 10. Dyadic communication is the earliest form of interaction we experience and the most common type of communication.

_____

_____

_____ 11. What qualifies as competent behavior in one culture might be completely inept, or even offensive, in another.

_____

_____

_____ 12. In order to build a competent relationship, we need to get rid of our need to maintain some space between ourselves and the other person.

_____

_____

_____ 13. You can build competent relationships only if you put the other person's needs ahead of yours.

_____

_____

Harcourt Brace & Company

_____ 14. Effective communicators are able to choose their actions from a wide range of behaviors.

_____

_____

_____ 15. Just knowing about communication skills makes you a better communicator.

_____

_____

COMPLETION

Fill in the blanks below with the correct terms chosen from the list below.

instrumental goals   social needs   identity needs   physiological noise
psychological noise   self-monitoring   control   commitment
cognitive complexity   empathy

1. _____ are the needs we have to define who we are.

2. _____ are the needs we have to link ourselves with others.

3. _____ are the needs we have to get others to behave in ways we want.

4. _____ refers to the forces within a communicator that interfere with the ability to express or understand a message accurately.

5. _____ refers to the biological factors in the receiver or sender that interfere with accurate reception of messages.

6. _____ is the degree to which the parties in a relationship have the power to influence one another.

7. _____ is the desire to interact and continue the relationship.

8. _____ is the ability to view issues in the relationship in a variety of different ways.

9. _____ is the process of paying close attention to your behavior in order to shape the way you behave.

10. _____ is the ability to take the other person's perspective in a relationship.

Harcourt Brace & Company

MULTIPLE CHOICE

Choose the letter of the communication process element that is most illustrated by the description found below. Italicized words provide clues.

a. encode
b. decode
c. channel
d. message/feedback
e. noise (external, physiological or psychological)
f. environment

_____ 1. The children make a *videotape* of themselves to send to their grandparents instead of writing a *letter*.

_____ 2. Marjorie tries to decide the best way to tell Martin that she can't go to Hawaii with him.

_____ 3. Martin decides Marjorie means she doesn't love him when she says she can't go to Hawaii.

_____ 4. It's so hot in the room that Brad has a hard time concentrating on what his partner is telling him.

_____ 5. Linda *smiles* while Larry is talking to her.

_____ 6. Brooke is daydreaming about her date while Allison is talking to her.

_____ 7. Since Jacob has never been married, it's difficult for him to understand why his married friend Brent wants to spend less time with him.

_____ 8. Whitney says, *"I'm positive about my vote."*

_____ 9. Richard *thinks* Jon wants to leave when he waves to him.

_____ 10. Laura *winks* when she *says* she's serious and *gestures* with her arms.

_____ 11. Erin is from a wealthy family and Kate from a poor one. They have a serious conflict about how to budget their money.

_____ 12. Jack has been feeling a cold coming on all day while he has sat through the meeting.

_____ 13. Levi constructs the best arguments to convince his parents to buy him a new car.

_____ 14. Jessica decides to lie to her group members about the reason she missed the meeting last night.

_____ 15. "I refuse to go," said Jeremy.

Harcourt Brace & Company

Choose the *best* answer for each of the questions below:

16. According to a contextual definition of interpersonal communication, interpersonal communication occurs when

    a. two people interact with one another, usually face to face.
    b. you watch a TV show about relationships.
    c. you read a romance novel.
    d. your romantic partner leaves a message on your answering machine.

17. All of the following statements are true <u>except</u>

    a. Communication can be intentional.
    b. Communication is irreversible.
    c. Communication can be unintentional.
    d. Communication is repeatable.

18. All of the following statements are true <u>except</u>

    a. Meanings are not in words.
    b. More communication is not always better.
    c. Communication can solve all your problems.
    d. Communication is not a natural ability.

19. The messages people exchange about their relationship are termed

    a. affinity.
    b. metacommunication.
    c. complementary symmetry.
    d. communication competence.

20. When you are able to perform communication skills without thinking about them, you have entered the skill stage of

    a. awareness.
    b. awkwardness.
    c. skillfulness.
    d. integration.

Harcourt Brace & Company

CHAPTER 1 STUDY GUIDE ANSWERS

MATCHING (KEY TERM REVIEW)

1.	d	5.	b	9.	j	13.	q	17.	t
2.	a	6.	c	10.	h	14.	l	18.	r
3.	g	7.	f	11.	p	15.	k	19.	o
4.	e	8.	i	12.	n	16.	m	20.	s

TRUE/FALSE

1.	T	4.	F	7.	F	10.	T	13.	F
2.	F	5.	T	8.	T	11.	T	14.	T
3.	F	6.	F	9.	F	12.	F	15.	F

COMPLETION

1. identity needs
2. social needs
3. instrumental goals
4. psychological noise
5. physiological noise
6. control
7. commitment
8. cognitive complexity
9. self-monitoring
10. empathy

MULTIPLE CHOICE

1.	c	5.	d	9.	b	13.	a	17.	d
2.	a	6.	e	10.	c	14.	a	18.	c
3.	b	7.	f	11.	f	15.	d	19.	b
4.	e	8.	d	12.	e	16.	a	20.	d

Harcourt Brace & Company

CHAPTER TWO

❖ Communication and the Self ❖

OUTLINE

Use this outline to take notes as you read the chapter in the text and/or as your instructor lectures in class.

I. COMMUNICATION AND THE SELF-CONCEPT
   A. Definition: The Relatively Stable Set of Perceptions You Hold of Yourself
   B. How the Self-Concept Develops
      1. Reflected appraisal (through significant others)
      2. Social comparison (through reference groups)
   C. Characteristics of the Self-Concept
      1. The self-concept is subjective
         a. Obsolete information
         b. Distorted feedback
         c. Emphasis on perfection
         d. Social expectations
      2. The self-concept resists change
         a. Change-not-acknowledged problem
         b. Self-delusion/lack of growth problem
   D. Culture and the Self-Concept
      1. Language
      2. Individualistic versus collective identities
   E. The Self-Fulfilling Prophecy and Communication
      1. Definition: expectations held that make an outcome more likely
      2. Types
         a. Self-imposed
         b. Imposed by others
      3. Influence
         a. Improve relationships
         b. Damage relationships
   F. Changing Your Self-Concept
      1. Have realistic expectations
      2. Have realistic perceptions
      3. Have the will to change
      4. Have the skill to change

II. PRESENTING THE SELF: COMMUNICATION AS IMPRESSION MANAGEMENT

    A. Public and Private Selves

        1. Perceived self

        2. Presenting self

           a. facework

           b. self-monitoring

    B. Why Manage Impressions?

        1. Social rules

        2. Personal goals

        3. Relational goals

    C. How Do We Manage Impressions?

        1. Manner

           a. Words

           b. Nonverbal behavior

        2. Appearance

        3. Setting

    D. Impression Management and Honesty

KEY TERMS

Use these key terms to review major concepts from your text. Write the definition for each key term in the space to the right

appearance _____

back _____

"can'ts" _____

cognitive conservatism _____

collective identity _____

distorted feedback _____

ego booster _____

ego buster _____

facework _____

front _____

ideal self _____

Harcourt Brace & Company

impression management _____

individualistic identity _____

manner _____

myth of perfection _____

obsolete information _____

perceived self _____

presenting self _____

reference groups _____

reflected appraisal _____

self-concept _____

self-fulfilling prophecy _____

self-monitor _____

self-verification _____

setting _____

significant other _____

social comparison _____

social expectations _____

"won'ts" _____

Harcourt Brace & Company

ACTIVITIES

❖ 2.1 WHO DO YOU THINK YOU ARE? ❖
◆ Activity Type: Invitation to Insight

PURPOSE
To help you identify your own self-concept.

INSTRUCTIONS
1. For each category below, supply the words or phrases that describe you best.
2. After filling in the spaces within each category, organize your responses so that the most fundamental characteristic is listed first, with the rest of the items following in order of descending importance.

PART A: IDENTIFY THE ELEMENTS OF YOUR SELF-CONCEPT

1. What moods or feelings best characterize you (cheerful, considerate, optimistic, etc.)?

    a. _____ b. _____ c. _____

2. How would you describe your physical condition and/or your appearance (tall, attractive, weak, muscular, etc.)?

    a. _____ b. _____ c. _____

3. How would you describe your social traits (friendly, shy, aloof, talkative, etc.)?

    a. _____ b. _____ c. _____

4. What talents do you possess or lack (good artist, lousy carpenter, competent swimmer, etc.)?

    a. _____ b. _____ c. _____

5. How would you describe your intellectual capacity (curious, poor reader, good mathematician, etc.)?

    a. _____ b. _____ c. _____

6. What beliefs do you hold strongly (vegetarian, Christian, passivist, etc.)?

    a. _____ b. _____ c. _____

7. What social roles are the most important in your life (brother, student, friend, bank teller, club president, etc.)?

a. _____ b. _____ c. _____

8. What other terms haven't you listed so far that describe other important things about yourself?

a. _____ b. _____ c. _____

PART B: ARRANGE YOUR SELF-CONCEPT ELEMENTS IN ORDER OF IMPORTANCE

1. _____ 13. _____

2. _____ 14. _____

3. _____ 15. _____

4. _____ 16. _____

5. _____ 17. _____

6. _____ 18. _____

7. _____ 19. _____

8. _____ 20. _____

9. _____ 21. _____

10. _____ 22. _____

11. _____ 23. _____

12. _____ 24. _____

❖ 2.2 EGO BOOSTERS AND BUSTERS ❖

◆ Activity Type: Invitation to Insight

PURPOSES

1. To help you identify how significant others have shaped your self-concept.
2. To help you realize how you shape the self-concept of others.

INSTRUCTIONS

1. In the appropriate spaces below describe the actions of several "ego boosters": significant others who shaped your self-concept in a positive way. Also describe the behavior of "ego busters" who contributed to a more negative self-concept.
2. Next, recall several incidents in which you behaved as an ego booster or buster to others. Not all ego boosters and busters are obvious. Include in your description several incidents in which the messages were subtle or nonverbal.
3. Summarize the lessons you have learned from this experience by answering the questions at the end of this exercise.

EGO BOOSTER MESSAGES YOU HAVE RECEIVED

EXAMPLE

I perceive(d) ___*my chem. lab partner*___ as telling me I am/was _____*attractive*_____ when he or she
               (significant other)   (self-concept element)

keeps (kept) sneaking glances at me and smiling during our experiments. _____

1. I perceive(d) _____ as telling me I am/was
                                (significant other)

_____ when he/she _____
     (self-concept element)

_____

_____

_____

2. I perceive(d) _____ as telling me I am/was
                                (significant other)

_____ when he/she _____
     (self-concept element)

_____

_____

_____

Harcourt Brace & Company

3. I perceive(d) _____ as telling me I am/was

_____ when he/she _____
(self-concept element)

_____

_____

EGO BUSTER MESSAGES YOU HAVE RECEIVED

EXAMPLE

I perceive(d) _*my neighbor*_ as telling me I am/was _*not an important friend*_ when he/she
(significant other)   (self-concept element)

*had a big party last weekend and didn't invite me.* _____

1. I perceive(d) _____ as telling me I am/was
(significant other)

_____ when he/she _____
(self-concept element)

_____

_____

2. I perceive(d) _____ as telling me I am/was
(significant other)

_____ when he/she _____
(self-concept element)

_____

_____

3. I perceive(d) _____ as telling me I am/was
(significant other)

_____ when he/she _____
(self-concept element)

_____

_____

EGO BOOSTER MESSAGES YOU HAVE SENT

EXAMPLE

I was a booster to___*my instructor*___ when I ___*told her I enjoyed last Tuesday's lecture.*___

1. I was a booster to _____ when I _____

   _____

   _____

2. I was a booster to _____ when I _____

   _____

   _____

   _____

3. I was a booster to _____ when I _____

   _____

   _____

EGO BUSTER MESSAGES YOU HAVE SENT

EXAMPLE

I was a buster to ___*my sister*___ when I ___*forgot to phone her or send even a card on her birthday.*___

1. I was a buster to _____ when I _____

   _____

   _____

2. I was a buster to _____ when I _____

   _____

   _____

3. I was a buster to _____ when I _____

   _____

   _____

Harcourt Brace & Company

CONCLUSIONS (USE AN ADDITIONAL SHEET OF PAPER IF NECESSARY)

Who are the people who have most influenced your self-concept in the past? What messages did each one send to influence you so strongly?

_____

_____

_____

_____

What people are the greatest influences on your self-concept now? Is each person a positive or a negative influence? What messages does each one send to influence your self-concept?

_____

_____

_____

_____

Who are the people whom _you_ have influenced most greatly? What messages have you sent to each one about his or her self-concept? How have you sent these messages?

_____

_____

_____

_____

What ego booster or buster messages do you want to send to the important people in your life? How can you send each one?

_____

_____

_____

_____

❖ 2.3 SELF-CONCEPT INVENTORY ❖

◆ Activity Type: Invitation to Insight

PURPOSE

1. To give you a clearer picture of how you see yourself (your perceived self).
2. To illustrate how others perceive you (presenting selves).

INSTRUCTIONS

1. Transfer the list of self-concept descriptors found below to index cards (or strips of paper, or carefully cut the ones on this page). Feel free to line out some descriptors or add those of your own.
2. Arrange your cards in a stack, with the one that *best* describes you at the top and the one that *least* describes you at the bottom.
3. Using the Perceived Self column (Table 1), record the order in which you arranged the cards (1 is the most like you). You will leave out some cards or add on to your list on the opposite page.
4. Cover your Perceived Self column and ask two other people (a friend, co-worker, roommate, family member, classmate) to arrange the descriptors in an order in which they see you. Record these perceptions in Tables 2 and 3, being sure to cover your own Table 1 and the Table 2 or 3 that the other person has worked on (so no one sees what the other has written). Record the name/relationship of your evaluator at the top of the appropriate column.
5. Compare the three tables, circling any descriptors that differ from column to column.
6. Answer the questions at the end of this exercise.

Intelligent	Constructive in personal relationships	Reliable
Shy	Satisfied with myself	Care about others
Express my feelings and ideas clearly	Comfortable in social situations	Tolerant
Give in easily	Confused	Honest with myself
Similar to other people	Friendly	Honest with others
Insecure	Emotionally mature	Make lots of excuses
Talk too much	Growing wiser over time	Avoid facing things
Helpful to others	Attractive	Good student and/or worker
Tense	Selfish	Athletic
Likable	Conscientious	Organized
Open-minded	Willing to stand up for beliefs	Neat

Table 1 Perceived Self	Table 2 Presenting Self to _____ (relationship to you)	Table 3 Presenting Self to _____ (relationship to you)
1. _____	1. _____	1. _____
2. _____	2. _____	2. _____
3. _____	3. _____	3. _____
4. _____	4. _____	4. _____
5. _____	5. _____	5. _____
6. _____	6. _____	6. _____
7. _____	7. _____	7. _____
8. _____	8. _____	8. _____
9. _____	9. _____	9. _____
10. _____	10. _____	10. _____
11. _____	11. _____	11. _____
12. _____	12. _____	12. _____
13. _____	13. _____	13. _____
14. _____	14. _____	14. _____
15. _____	15. _____	15. _____
16. _____	16. _____	16. _____
17. _____	17. _____	17. _____
18. _____	18. _____	18. _____
19. _____	19. _____	19. _____
20. _____	20. _____	20. _____
21. _____	21. _____	21. _____
22. _____	22. _____	22. _____
23. _____	23. _____	23. _____
24. _____	24. _____	24. _____

Describe any factors that have contributed in a positive or negative way to the formation of your perceived self (obsolete information, social expectations, perfectionistic beliefs). Include any other factors involved in the formation of your perceived self (for example, certain significant others, any strong reference groups).

_____

_____

_____

_____

_____

Describe any differences between your perceived self and the ways your evaluators perceived you (your presenting selves). What factors contribute to the differences in perception? Whose view is the most accurate and why?

_____

_____

_____

_____

_____

Why might your partners in this exercise view you differently from the way you perceive yourself? Would other people in your life view you like either of the people in this exercise? Give some specific examples with reasons why they would or would not have a similar perception.

_____

_____

_____

_____

_____

Harcourt Brace & Company

✛ 2.4 REEVALUATING YOUR "CAN'TS" ✛

◆ **Activity Type: Invitation to Insight**

PURPOSE

To help you identify and eliminate any self-fulfilling prophecies which hamper effective communication.

INSTRUCTIONS

1. Complete the following lists by describing communication-related difficulties you have in the following areas.
2. After filling in each blank space, follow the starred instructions that follow the list (*).

DIFFICULTIES YOU HAVE COMMUNICATING WITH FAMILY MEMBERS

EXAMPLES

I can't *discuss politics with my dad without having an argument* _____
because *he's so set in his ways.* _____
I can't *tell my brother how much I love him* _____
because *I'll feel foolish.* _____

1. I can't _____

   because _____

2. I can't _____

   because _____

* Corrections (see instructions at end of exercise)

_____

_____

DIFFICULTIES YOU HAVE COMMUNICATING WITH PEOPLE AT SCHOOL OR AT WORK

EXAMPLES

I can't *say "no" when my boss asks me to work overtime* _____
because *he'll fire me.*
I can't *participate in class discussions even when I know the answers or have a question* _____
because *I just freeze up.* _____

1. I can't _____

   because _____

2. I can't _____

   because _____

* Corrections (see instructions at end of exercise)

_____

_____

DIFFICULTIES YOU HAVE COMMUNICATING WITH STRANGERS

EXAMPLES
I can't *start a conversation with someone I've never met before*
because *I'll look stupid.*
I can't *ask smokers to move or stop smoking*
because *they'll get mad.*

1. I can't _____

   because _____

2. I can't _____

   because _____

* Corrections (see instructions at end of exercise)

_____

_____

DIFFICULTIES YOU HAVE COMMUNICATING WITH FRIENDS

EXAMPLES
I can't *find the courage to ask my friend to repay the money he owes me*
because *I'm afraid he'll question our friendship.*
I can't *say no when friends ask me to do favors and I'm busy*
because *I'm afraid they'll think I'm not their friend.*

1. I can't _____

   because _____

2. I can't _____

   because _____

* Corrections (see instructions at end of exercise)

_____

_____

Harcourt Brace & Company

*After you have completed the list, continue as follows:

a. Read the list you have made. Actually say each item to yourself and note your feelings.

b. Now read the list again, but with a slight difference. For each "can't," substitute the word "won't." For instance, "I can't say no to friends' requests" becomes "I won't say no." Circle any statements that are actually "won'ts."

c. Read the list for a third time. For this repetition substitute "I don't know how" for your original "can't." Instead of saying "I can't approach strangers," say, "I don't know how to approach strangers." *Correct* your original list to show which statements are truly "don't know hows."

After completing this exercise, you should be more aware of the power that negative self-fulfilling prophecies have on your self-concept and thus on your communication behavior. Imagine how differently you would behave if you eliminated any incorrect uses of the word "can't" from your thinking.

Harcourt Brace & Company

✤ 2.5 YOUR SELF-FULFILLING PROPHECIES ✤

◆❖ Activity Type: Skill Builder

PURPOSES

1. To help you identify the self-fulfilling prophecies you impose on yourself.
2. To help you identify the self-fulfilling prophecies others impose on you.

INSTRUCTIONS

1. Identify three communication-related, self-fulfilling prophecies you impose on yourself. For each, identify the item, describe the prediction you make, and show how this prediction influences either your behavior or that of others.
2. Next, identify two communication-related, self-fulfilling prophecies others have imposed on you. For each, show how the other person's prediction affected your behavior.

PROPHECIES YOU IMPOSE ON YOURSELF

EXAMPLE

Item *Inept in social situations*

Prediction *When I'm at a party or other social gathering, I think about how foolish I'll sound when I meet strangers.*

Outcome *I do sound foolish when I meet them. I stammer, avoid eye contact, and can't think of anything interesting to say.*

How your prediction affected outcome *I think that expecting to fail causes me to sound foolish. If I didn't expect to sound so foolish, I'd probably behave with more confidence.*

1. Item _____

    Prediction _____

    _____

    _____

    Outcome _____

    _____

    _____

    How prediction affected outcome _____

    _____

    _____

Harcourt Brace & Company

2. Item _____

   Prediction _____

   _____

   _____

   Outcome _____

   _____

   _____

   How prediction affected outcome _____

   _____

   _____

3. Item _____

   Prediction _____

   _____

   _____

   Outcome _____

   _____

   _____

   How prediction affected outcome _____

   _____

   _____

PROPHECIES OTHERS IMPOSE ON YOU

EXAMPLE

Item *Good listener*

Prediction *My friends often share their problems with me and tell me that I'm a good listener.*

Outcome *I'm willing to listen in the future.*

How your prediction affected outcome *Being told I'm a good listener makes me more willing to I lend an ear. If they told me I was no help, I'd probably discourage them from bringing me their problems in the future.*

1. Item _____

   Prediction _____

   _____

   _____

   Outcome _____

   _____

   _____

   How prediction affected outcome _____

   _____

   _____

2. Item _____

   Prediction _____

   _____

   _____

   Outcome _____

   _____

   _____

   How prediction affected outcome _____

   _____

   _____

Harcourt Brace & Company

✛ 2.6 SUCCESS IN MANAGING IMPRESSIONS ✛

❖ Activity Type: Skill Builder

PURPOSES

1. To acknowledge at least one successful face that you have revealed to others.
2. To reflect on your level of self-monitoring in that instance.
3. To listen to the successful "faces" of others.

INSTRUCTIONS

1. In groups, describe to one another one instance in which each of you has successfully presented yourself to another person. Describe how you managed that impression of yourself. It may be a significant impression (you got a job you wanted or a date you wanted) or it may be an ongoing, slowly made success (you were a better parent this week or you kept your cool with your roommate during last week's conflict). Describe how you managed manner, setting and/or appearance to create the impression you wanted.
2. Describe to others how aware you were of your own behaviors. Describe whether you had high or low self-monitoring, and how effective or ineffective your level of monitoring was for the impression management situation.
3. Listen to the examples of others as you get to know people in your group.

The successful face I revealed to others

_____

_____

_____

_____

_____

Effectiveness of self-monitoring

_____

_____

_____

_____

_____

Impressions I received from listening to others

_____

_____

_____

_____

_____

STUDY GUIDE

CHECK YOUR UNDERSTANDING

MATCHING (KEY TERM REVIEW)

Match the terms in column 1 with their definitions in column 2.

_____ 1. back

_____ 2. face

_____ 3. facework

_____ 4. front

_____ 5. cognitive conservatism

_____ 6. ideal self

_____ 7. impression management

_____ 8. perceived self

_____ 9. presenting self

_____ 10. reference groups

_____ 11. reflected appraisal

_____ 12. self-concept

_____ 13. self-fulfilling prophecy

_____ 14. significant other

_____ 15. social comparison

_____ 16. collective identity

_____ 17. individualistic identity

_____ 18. self-verification

_____ 19. self-monitoring

_____ 20. obsolete information

a. the relatively stable set of perceptions each individual holds of himself or herself

b. the region in which behavior will not be perceived by an audience

c. strategies used by communicators to influence the way others view them

d. the image a person presents to others

e. the person each wishes to be

f. the theory that a person's self-concept matches the way the person believes others regard him or her

g. verbal and nonverbal behavior designed to create and maintain a communicator's face and the face of others

h. the socially approved identity that a communicator tries to present

i. groups against which we compare ourselves, thereby influencing our self-concept and self-esteem

j. publicly visible behavior

k. the tendency to seek and attend to information that conforms to an existing self-concept

l. the person we believe ourselves to be in moments of candor

m. evaluation of oneself in terms of or by comparison to others

n. a self-concept that is strongly "I" oriented, common in cultures where the main desire is to promote the self

o. the tendency to look for people who confirm our self-concept

p. past successes or failures that no longer hold true for the self

q. a person whose opinion is important enough to affect one's self-concept strongly

r. a self-concept that is highly dependent on belonging to a group, common in cultures where the main desire is to build connections between the self and others

s. the process of attending to one's behavior and using these observations to shape the way one behaves

t. a prediction or expectation of an event that makes the outcome more likely to occur than would otherwise have been the case

Harcourt Brace & Company

TRUE/FALSE

Mark the statements below as true or false. Correct statements that are false on the lines below to create a true statement.

_____ 1. Every aspect of your self-concept is equally important.

_____

_____

_____ 2. Most researchers agree that we are not born with a self-concept.

_____

_____

_____ 3. The influence of significant others becomes less powerful as we grow older.

_____

_____

_____ 4. People who dislike themselves are likely to believe that others won't like them either.

_____

_____

_____ 5. Research has shown that people with high self-esteem seek out partners who view them unfavorably because they are strong enough to take the criticism.

_____

_____

_____ 6. Luckily, your self-concept is not affected by the language that you speak.

_____

_____

_____ 7. In individualistic societies, there is a higher degree of communication apprehension.

_____

_____

Harcourt Brace & Company

_____ 8. The self-concept is such a powerful force on the personality that it not only determines how you see yourself in the present but also can actually influence your future behavior and that of others.

_____

_____

_____ 9. Research shows that people who believe they are incompetent are more likely than others to pursue rewarding relationships in an attempt to ally themselves with competent people.

_____

_____

_____ 10. The communication strategies we use to influence how others view us are all conscious behaviors.

_____

_____

COMPLETION

Fill in the blanks below with the correct terms chosen from the list below.

distorted feedback   obsolete information   self-delusion
ego booster   ego buster   realistic expectations
realistic perceptions   manner   setting
appearance

1. _____ is someone who helps enhance your self-esteem by acting in ways that make you feel accepted, important and loved.

2. _____ is someone who acts to reduce your self-esteem.

3. _____ are messages that others send to you that are unrealistically positive or negative.

4. _____ consists of a communicator's words and nonverbal actions that help create a front.

5. _____ is information that was once true about you that is no longer true.

6. _____ are the personal items people use to shape an image.

7. _____ is the inability to see a real need for change in the self due to holding an unrealistically favorable picture of yourself.

8. _____ are reasonable goals to set for self-growth.

9. _____ refers to the physical items we use to influence how others view us.

10. _____ are relatively accurate views of the strengths and weaknesses of the self.

MULTIPLE CHOICE

Identify which principle influences the self-concept in each example. Place the letter of the correct term on the line adjacent to each description.

a. obsolete information
b. distorted feedback
c. emphasis on perfection
d. social expectations

_____ 1. You always scored more points than anyone else on your team in high school. You still think you're the best even though your college teammates are scoring more than you.

_____ 2. You keep getting down on yourself because you can't cook as well as Megan, even though you are a great student and a fair athlete.

_____ 3. You tell everyone how you "blew" the chemistry test and got a "C–" but you don't ever acknowledge your "A's" in math.

_____ 4. Your parents tell you, their friends, and all your relatives about all your wonderful accomplishments, even though you have only average achievement.

_____ 5. Janee says that you are insensitive to her perspective despite your many attempts to listen honestly to her and empathize.

_____ 6. You pay a lot of attention to the magazines showing perfectly dressed and groomed individuals and keep wishing you could look as good as they do.

_____ 7. You think of yourself as the shy fifth grader despite being at the social hub of at least three clubs on campus.

_____ 8. You feel uncomfortable accepting the compliments your friends honestly give you.

_____ 9. You're exhausted by trying to get all A's, work 30 hours a week, and be a loving romantic partner at the same time. You don't see how so many other people manage to get it all done.

_____ 10. "You're the perfect weight," your father tells you despite your recent gain of twenty pounds over the normal weight for your height.

Choose the *best* answer for each statement below:

11. Deciding which face—which part of you—to reveal is termed

a. frontwork.
b. impression management.
c. hypocrisy.
d. two-faced syndrome.

12. The most significant part of a person's self-concept

    a. is the social roles the person plays.
    b. is his or her appearance.
    c. is his or her accomplishments.
    d. will vary from person to person.

13. The self-concept begins to

    a. at conception.
    b. in the womb.
    c. during the first year of life.
    d. at the onset of puberty.

14. Which of the following could be an example of a self-fulfilling prophecy?

    a. Sid is born with a very large nose.
    b. Marguerita has a very large, extended family.
    c. Serge is a Russian immigrant.
    d. Joy has given up on trying to talk to her unreasonable father.

15. The fact that none of us can see ourselves completely accurately illustrates the _____ nature of the self-concept.

    a. subjective
    b. objective
    c. unrealistic
    d. verification

Harcourt Brace & Company

CHAPTER 2 STUDY GUIDE ANSWERS

MATCHING (KEY TERM REVIEW)

1. b	5. k	9. d	13. t	17. n
2. h	6. e	10. i	14. q	18. o
3. g	7. c	11. f	15. m	19. s
4. j	8. l	12. a	16. r	20. p

TRUE/FALSE

1. F	5. F	9. F
2. T	6. F	10. F
3. T	7. F	
4. T	8. T	

COMPLETION

1. ego booster
2. ego buster
3. distorted feedback
4. manner
5. obsolete information
6. appearance
7. self-delusion
8. realistic expectations
9. setting
10. realistic perceptions

MULTIPLE CHOICE

1. a	4. b	7. a	10. b	13. c
2. c	5. b	8. d	11. b	14. d
3. d	6. c	9. c	12. d	15. a

Harcourt Brace & Company

✚ Perception: What You See Is What You Get ✚

OUTLINE

Use this outline to take notes as you read the chapter in the text and/or as your instructor lectures in class.

I. **THE PERCEPTION PROCESS**
  A. **Selection**
    1. Factors that influence selection
      a. Intense stimuli
      b. Repetitious stimuli
      c. Contrast or change in stimulation
      d. Motives
    2. Distortions in selection
      a. Omission
      b. Oversimplification
  B. **Organization**
    1. Figure–ground organization
    2. Perceptual schema
      a. Physical constructs
      b. Role constructs
      c. Interaction constructs
      d. Psychological constructs
      e. Membership constructs
    3. Effects of organization
      a. Stereotyping
      b. Punctuation
  C. **Interpretation—Factors That Influence**
    1. Relational satisfaction
    2. Degree of involvement with the other person
    3. Past experience
    4. Assumptions about human behavior
    5. Expectations
    6. Knowledge
    7. Personal mood

II. INFLUENCES ON PERCEPTION

   A. **Physiological**

      1. Senses
      2. Age
      3. Health
      4. Fatigue
      5. Hunger
      6. Biological Cycles

   B. **Cultural**

      1. Language translations
      2. Nonverbal behaviors
      3. Value of talk
      4. Ethnicity
      5. Geography

   C. **Social Roles**

   D. **Gender Roles**

   E. **Occupational Roles**

   F. **Self-Concept**

      1. Judgments of others
      2. Judgments of self

III. THE ACCURACY—AND INACCURACY—OF PERCEPTION

   A. **We Often Judge Ourselves More Charitably Than Others**

   B. **We Are Influenced by What Is Most Obvious**

   C. **We Cling to First Impressions**

   D. **We Tend to Assume Others Are Similar to Us**

IV. PERCEPTION CHECKING TO PREVENT MISUNDERSTANDINGS

   A. **Elements of Perception Checking**

      1. Describe behavior
      2. Interpret behavior two ways
      3. Request clarification

   B. **Perception-Checking Considerations**

      1. Completeness
      2. Nonverbal congruency
      3. Cultural rules
         a. Low-context cultures
         b. High-context cultures

Harcourt Brace & Company

V. EMPATHY AND COMMUNICATION

   A. **Definition**
      1. Empathy—ability to re-create another's perspective
         a. Perspective taking
         b. Emotional dimension
         c. Genuine concern
      2. Sympathy—compassion for another's predicament
   B. **The Pillow Method—A Tool for Building Empathy**
      1. Position One: I'm right, you're wrong
      2. Position Two: You're right, I'm wrong
      3. Position Three: Both right, both wrong
      4. Position Four: The issue isn't as important as it seems
      5. Conclusion: There is truth in all four perspectives

KEY TERMS

Use these key terms to review major concepts from your text. Write the definition for each key term in the space to the right

androgynous _____

attribution _____

cultural differences _____

empathy _____

figure–ground organization _____

gender roles _____

high-context culture _____

interaction constructs _____

interpretation _____

low-context culture _____

membership constructs _____

occupational roles _____

omission _____

organization _____

Harcourt Brace & Company

oversimplification _____

perception _____

perception checking _____

perceptual schema _____

physical constructs _____

physiological influences _____

pillow method _____

psychological constructs _____

punctuation _____

role constructs _____

selection _____

self-serving bias _____

social roles _____

stereotyping _____

subcultural differences _____

sympathy _____

Harcourt Brace & Company

ACTIVITIES

❖ 3.1 GUARDING AGAINST PERCEPTUAL ERRORS ❖

◆ Activity Type: Invitation to Insight

PURPOSES

1. To help you identify potentially distorted opinions you have formed about people.
2. To help you recognize some perceptual errors that may have contributed to those distorted opinions.

INSTRUCTIONS

1. Identify two people about whom you've formed strong opinions. These opinions can be positive or negative. In either case, describe them.
2. Using the checklist provided, comment on the accuracy or inaccuracy of your perceptions of each person. See Chapter 3 of *Looking Out/Looking In* for a more detailed description of the checklist factors. NOTE: Not every factor may apply to each person.
3. Record your conclusions at the end of the exercise.
4. Compare your examples with those of other classmates.

	Example	Person A	Person B
Identify each person. Describe your opinions.	Joni is my wife's good friend. I don't like her; I think she's inconsiderate and selfish and boring. Her voice is shrill and I find her annoying.		
1. We are influenced by what is most obvious.	Because she is my wife's friend, Joni is around a lot, and it seems that I am always noticing her voice or her calls—perhaps I'm looking for them.		
2. We cling to first impressions, even if wrong.	I haven't liked Joni from the beginning. She always used to call right at our dinner time. Even though she doesn't do this anymore, I still remember it and I'm influenced by it.		

		Example	Person A	Person B
3.	We tend to assume others are similar to us.			
4.	We judge ourselves more charitably than others.	When Joni lost her job, I thought it was Joni's fault because she's so annoying. Of course, when I got laid off a few months later, I complained heavily about the economy and knew being laid off had nothing to do with my performance or personality.		

CONCLUSIONS

Based on the observations above, how accurate or inaccurate are your perceptions of other people?

_____

_____

_____

_____

What might you do in the future to guard against inaccurate perceptions of people?

_____

_____

_____

_____

Harcourt Brace & Company

✜ 3.2 EXAMINING YOUR INTERPRETATIONS ✜

◆ **Activity Type: Invitation to Insight**

PURPOSES

1. To help you identify the interpretations you make about others' behavior in your important interpersonal relationships.
2. To help you recognize the perceptual factors that influence those assumptions.
3. To help you consider the validity of your interpretations.

INTRODUCTION

There are many ways to interpret what another person says or does. For example, you may notice that a new classmate is wearing a cross necklace and imagine that she is a religious person, or you might notice that a friend isn't making much eye contact with you and assume that he is not telling you the truth.

We usually assume that our interpretations are accurate. In fact, these assumptions might be incorrect or quite different from how the other person sees himself or herself.

INSTRUCTIONS

1. For the next few days, observe three people and use the spaces below to record your interpretations of each.
2. After completing the information below, share your observations with each person involved and see if your interpretations match the explanations of each subject.

EXAMPLE

Name _Stan Morris_____   context _Neighbor and friend_____

A. Describe an assumption about this person's thoughts or feelings.
   I've been thinking that Stan is mad at me, probably because I've been asking so many favors of him lately.

B. Describe at least two items of behavior (things the person has said or done) that lead you to believe your assumption about this person's thoughts or feelings is accurate.
   1. *When I asked to borrow his backpacking gear he said yes, but he mentioned several times how much it cost him.*
   2. *When I asked him for a ride to school last week when my car was in the shop, he said OK but didn't talk much and drove more quickly than usual.*

C. Give at least two reasons why your assumption about this person's thoughts or feelings may *not* be accurate. (You may ask the person you are observing for help.)
   1. *Stan is often a moody person. Even if he is upset, it may not be because of anything I've said or done.*
   2. *I'm often hard on myself, taking the blame for anything that goes wrong. Perhaps I'm doing that here, and Stan doesn't mind doing me the favors.*

Harcourt Brace & Company

D. Which of the following factors influenced your perception of this person? Explain how each of these factors affected the accuracy or inaccuracy of your interpretations.

Physiological influences _____

_____

_____

Sex/occupational roles *Perhaps my being a woman has something to do with my self-doubt. I often wonder if I'm being too "forward" in asking a man for favors.*

Cultural/subcultural roles _____

_____

_____

Self-concept *I often view myself as less desirable as a friend than other people I know. I think this leads me to interpret others' reactions as confirmations of my worst fears, whether or not those fears are valid.*

PERSON 1

Name _____ Context _____

A. Describe an assumption you have made about this person's thoughts or feelings.

_____

_____

_____

B. Describe at least two items of behavior (things the person has said or done) that lead you to believe your assumption about this person's thoughts or feelings is accurate.

1. _____

_____

_____

2. _____

_____

_____

Harcourt Brace & Company

C. Give at least two reasons why your assumption about this person's thoughts or feelings may *not* be accurate. (You may ask the person you are observing for help.)

1. _____

    _____

    _____

2. _____

    _____

    _____

D. Which of the following factors influence your perception of this person? Explain how each of these factors affected the accuracy or inaccuracy of your interpretations.

Physiological influences _____

_____

_____

Sex/occupational roles _____

_____

_____

Cultural/subcultural roles _____

_____

_____

Self-concept _____

_____

_____

PERSON 2

Name _____ Context _____

A. Describe an assumption you have made about this person's thoughts or feelings.

_____

_____

_____

Harcourt Brace & Company

B. Describe at least two items of behavior (things the person has said or done) that lead you to
    believe your assumption about this person's thoughts or feelings is accurate.

    1. _____

        _____

        _____

    2. _____

        _____

        _____

C. Give at least two reasons why your assumption about this person's thoughts or feelings
    may *not* be accurate. (You may ask the person you are observing for help.)

    1. _____

        _____

        _____

    2. _____

        _____

        _____

D. Which of the following factors influenced your perception of this person? Explain how each
    of these factors affected the accuracy or inaccuracy of your interpretations.

    Physiological influences _____

    _____

    _____

    Sex/occupational roles _____

    _____

    _____

    Cultural/subcultural roles _____

    _____

    _____

Harcourt Brace & Company

Self-concept _____

_____

_____

PERSON 3

Name _____ Context _____

A. Describe an assumption you have made about this person's thoughts or feelings.

_____

_____

_____

B. Describe at least two items of behavior (things the person has said or done) that lead you to believe your assumption about this person's thoughts or feelings is accurate.

1. _____

_____

2. _____

_____

_____

C. Give at least two reasons why your assumption about this person's thoughts or feelings may *not* be accurate. (You may ask the person you are observing for help.)

1. _____

_____

_____

2. _____

_____

_____

Harcourt Brace & Company

D. Which of the following factors influenced your perception of this person? Explain how each of these factors affected the accuracy or inaccuracy of your interpretations.

Physiological influences _____

_____

_____

Sex/occupational roles _____

_____

_____

Cultural/subcultural roles _____

_____

_____

Self-concept _____

_____

_____

Harcourt Brace & Company

✤ 3.3 SHIFTING PERSPECTIVES (PILLOW METHOD) ✤

◆ **Activity Type: Invitation to Insight**

PURPOSES

1. To help you understand how others view an interpersonal issue.
2. To help you recognize the merits and drawbacks of each person's perspective.
3. To help you recognize how an interpersonal issue may not be as important as it first seems.

INSTRUCTIONS

1. Select one disagreement or other issue that is now affecting an interpersonal relationship.
2. Record enough background information for an outsider to understand the issue. Who is involved? How long has the disagreement been going on? What are the basic issues involved?
3. Describe the issue from each of the four positions listed below.
4. Record your conclusions at the end of this exercise.

OPTION

With a partner, role-play your situation orally, using 3.8 *Pillow Method*.

Background Information

_____

_____

_____

_____

_____

_____

Position 1: Explain how you are right and the other person is wrong.

_____

_____

_____

_____

_____

_____

Harcourt Brace & Company

Position 2: Explain how the other person's position is correct, or at least understandable.

_____

_____

_____

_____

_____

Position 3: Show that there are both correct (or understandable) and mistaken (or unreasonable) parts of both positions.

_____

_____

_____

_____

_____

Position 4: Describe at least two ways in which the elements developed in positions 1–3 might affect your relationship. Describe at least one way in which the issue might be seen as *less* important than it was originally and describe at least one way in which the issue might be seen as *more* important than it was originally.

_____

_____

_____

_____

_____

_____

Harcourt Brace & Company

CONCLUSION

Explain how there is some truth in each of the preceding positions. Also explain how viewing the issue from each of the preceding positions has changed your perception of the issue and how it may change your behavior in the future. Explain how this issue and your understanding of it affect your relationship.

_____

_____

_____

_____

_____

❖ 3.4 OBSERVATION AND PERCEPTION ❖

❖ Activity Type: Skill Builder

PURPOSES

1. To report your observations of another person clearly and accurately.
2. To report at least two interpretations about the meaning of your observations to another person.
3. To discuss and evaluate the various choices you have available to you when dealing with perceptual problems.

INSTRUCTIONS

1. As a group, detail three situations below in which there are potential perceptual problems.
2. Use the form below to record behavior for each relationship listed.
3. For each example of behavior, record two plausible interpretations.
4. Record a request for feedback.
5. With others in the group, rehearse how you could share with the person in question each example of behavior and the possible interpretations you have developed.
6. Evaluate the various other options you have to check out perceptions. Describe the probable outcome of each.

EXAMPLE

Perceptual problem: *Jill's math professor is really annoying her—calling on her for answers and trying to get her involved more in the class. Jill is uncomfortable about this, but she is afraid that the professor might pay even more attention to her if she brings it up.*

Perception checking statement: *Professor Smith, I'm confused about something.*

Behavior: *I've noticed that you call on me quite often—at least once each class, whether or not I raise my hand.*

Interpretation A: *Sometimes I wonder if you're trying to catch me unprepared.*

Interpretation B: *On the other hand, sometimes I think you're trying to challenge me by forcing me to keep on my toes.*

Request for feedback: *Can you tell me why you call on me so often?*

Perception checking options

1. *Jill could do nothing. Perhaps it would be better to wait and see if she has been imagining this by watching a bit more.*
2. *Jill could start initiating answers herself and see if Professor Smith changes behavior.*
3. *Jill could just tell the Prof that she doesn't like being called on. This might alienate her in the Prof's eyes, however, and might affect her grade.*
4. *Jill could just ask if the Prof was trying to embarrass her. We thought the Prof might not know what Jill was referring to, though, if she didn't describe behavior. The Prof probably teaches hundreds of students and might not realize what's going on in Jill's eyes.*
5. *Jill could do the complete perception checking statement we wrote above. Our group thought this has a good chance for success if the Prof didn't get defensive. If Jill could deliver the statement in a non-defensive tone and then follow it up with how much she likes the class, perhaps the Prof would realize how much Jill is bothered.*

Harcourt Brace & Company

SITUATION ONE

Perceptual problem: _____

_____

_____

Perception-checking statement: _____

   Behavior: _____

   Interpretation A: _____

   Interpretation B: _____

   Request for feedback: _____

Perception-checking options:

_____

_____

_____

_____

_____

SITUATION TWO

Perceptual problem: _____

_____

_____

Perception-checking statement: _____

   Behavior: _____

   Interpretation A: _____

   Interpretation B: _____

   Request for feedback: _____

Harcourt Brace & Company

Perception-checking options:

_____

_____

_____

_____

_____

SITUATION THREE

Perceptual problem: _____

_____

_____

Perception-checking statement: _____

   Behavior: _____

   Interpretation A: _____

   Interpretation B: _____

   Request for feedback: _____

Perception-checking options:

_____

_____

_____

_____

_____

Harcourt Brace & Company

✜ 3.5 APPLYING PERCEPTION CHECKING ✜

◆❖ Activity Type: Skill Builder

PURPOSE

To prepare , deliver, and evaluate effective perception-checking statements.

INSTRUCTIONS

1. Choose two people with whom you have relational concerns. Give careful consideration to the partners you choose, choose concerns that are real and important, and allow yourself enough time to discuss your concerns with each partner.
2. Identify the concern, its importance to you, and consider the best time and place to approach each person.
3. Prepare perception-checking statements to deliver to each person.
4. Deliver your perception statements, discussing with each person your understanding of his or her behavior and the accuracy or inaccuracy of your perceptions. OR discuss why you decided not to use perception checking in this situation—and what you did alternately.

PARTNER 1

PART ONE: DESCRIBE YOUR CONCERN

Partner's name _____

A. Describe your primary concern. _____

_____

_____

B. Why is it important to you to clarify this matter? _____

_____

_____

C. When and where is the best time to talk with this person? _____

_____

_____

Harcourt Brace & Company

PART TWO: PREPARING YOUR PERCEPTION-CHECKING STATEMENT

A.   Describe your observations of the other person's behavior. _____

_____

_____

B.   Write one interpretation that you believe could explain the behaviors you have observed.

_____

_____

_____

C.   Now write a second interpretation that is distinctly different from your previous one and
     which you believe could also explain the behavior you have observed.

_____

_____

_____

D.   Make a request for feedback. _____

PART THREE: SHARING YOUR PERCEPTION-CHECKING STATEMENT

Meet with your partner and (1) share your description of this person's behavior, (2) explain both
of your interpretations of the behavior, and (3) ask your partner to react to the interpretations you
have shared.

Describe the outcome of your conversation with your partner. _____

_____

_____

_____

OR, if you think perception checking would not be appropriate or effective, explain why you
decided not to use perception checking in this situation—and what you did alternately.

_____

_____

_____

_____

Harcourt Brace & Company

PARTNER 2

PART ONE: DESCRIBE YOUR CONCERN

Partner's name _____

A. Describe your primary concern. _____

_____

_____

B. Why is it important to you to clarify this matter? _____

_____

_____

C. When and where is the best time to talk with this person? _____

_____

_____

PART TWO: PREPARING YOUR PERCEPTION-CHECKING STATEMENT

A. Describe your observations of the other person's behavior. _____

_____

_____

B. Write one interpretation that you believe could explain the behaviors you have observed.

_____

_____

_____

C. Now write a second interpretation which is distinctly different from your previous one and which you believe could also explain the behavior you have observed.

_____

_____

_____

D. Make a request for feedback. _____

Harcourt Brace & Company

PART THREE: SHARING YOUR PERCEPTION-CHECKING STATEMENT

Meet with your partner and (1) share your description of this person's behavior, (2) explain both of your interpretations of the behavior, and (3) ask your partner to react to the interpretations you have shared.

Describe the outcome of your conversation with your partner. _____

_____

_____

_____

OR, if you think perception checking would not be appropriate or effective, explain why you decided not to use perception checking in this situation—and what you did alternately.

_____

_____

_____

_____

SUMMARY

1.   How accurate were your interpretations in the two situations above?

_____

_____

_____

2.   Based on your experiences in this exercise, in what circumstances are your interpretations accurate? When are they likely to be inaccurate? Consider the people involved, the topic of communication, and your personal moods and thoughts.

_____

_____

_____

_____

Harcourt Brace & Company

3. How did your partners react when you communicated by using perception checking? How did these reactions differ from the reactions you get when you jump to conclusions instead of using perception checking? If you decided not to use perception checking, what did you do instead and what were the results? How could this improve your relationships in the future?

_____

_____

_____

_____

4. Based on your experience in this exercise, when and how can you use perception checking in your everyday communication? With whom? In what situations? What difference will using perception checking make in your interpersonal relationships?

_____

_____

_____

_____

❖ 3.6 PERCEPTION-CHECKING PRACTICE ❖

❖ **Activity Type: Skill Builder**

PURPOSE

To create effective perception-checking statements.

INSTRUCTIONS

OPTION A:
Practice writing perception-checking statements for items 1–10 below.

OPTION B:
1. Join with a partner to create a dyad. Label one person A and the other B.
2. Both A and B should write perception-checking statements for items 1–10 below.
3. A then delivers items 1–5 to B orally. B should use Evaluation Form 3.7 to rate A's responses for these items.
4. B delivers items 6–10 orally to A. A should use Checklist 3.7 to rate B's responses for these items.

OPTION C:
Practice items 1–10 below orally with a partner. Deliver your best perception check in class while your instructor evaluates you.

EXAMPLE
Yesterday you saw your friend walking on the beach engaged in what looked to you like an intense conversation with your recent date, Chris.

Perception-checking statement *When I saw you yesterday walking on the beach with Chris, I didn't know what to make of it. I thought you might be talking about that class you're taking together, but I also wondered whether you're interested in dating Chris. Are you interested in Chris as a friend, or as a date?*

1. During last week's exam you thought you saw your friend Jim, who sits next to you in class, looking at your paper.

_____
_____
_____

2. Ever since the school year began, members of your family have made a point of asking how you are doing several times each month. They have just asked again.

_____
_____
_____

3. Your friend Carlo was driving you home from a party last night when he began to weave the car between lanes on the highway. You were uncomfortable, but didn't say anything then. Now it is the next morning and Carlo shows up to take you to a class. You have decided to bring up the incident.

_____

_____

_____

4. Last month you had a long talk with your friend Rachelle about her troubled engagement. Now you run into her in the shopping mall, and she talks for ten minutes about what she is doing without mentioning her fiancé.

_____

_____

_____

5. You return home at night to find your roommate, Tom, reading on the couch. When you walk into the room and greet Tom, he grunts and turns his face away from you and keeps reading.

_____

_____

_____

6. Last week your instructor, Dr. Green, returned your exam with a low grade and the comment, "This kind of work paints a bleak picture for the future." You have approached him to discuss the remark.

_____

_____

_____

7. In one of your regular long distance phone conversations you ask your favorite cousin, Mike, about the state of his up-and-down romantic life. He sighs and says, "Oh, it's OK, I guess."

_____

_____

_____

Harcourt Brace & Company

8. Your girl or boyfriend (or spouse) announces that she or he plans to spend next Friday night with friends from work. You usually spend Friday nights alone together.

_____

_____

_____

9. Last week your supervisor at work, Ms. White, gave you a big assignment. Three times since then she has asked you whether you're having any trouble with it.

_____

_____

_____

10. Last weekend your next-door neighbor, Steve, raked a big pile of leaves near your property line, promising to clean them up after work on Monday. It's Wednesday, and the wind is blowing the leaves into your yard.

_____

_____

_____

11. One of your classmates sits by you every day in class and runs after you to walk across campus; now he has started calling you at home every evening. He now suggests that you do some things on the weekend together.

_____

_____

_____

12. You've noticed one of your office mates looking over at you a number of times during the past few days. At first she looked away quickly, but now she smiles every time you look up and catch her looking at you. You've been under a lot of pressure at work lately and have been extremely busy. You can't understand why she keeps looking at you. You've decided to ask.

_____

_____

_____

Harcourt Brace & Company

13. It seems that every time you have been leaving your house lately, your roommate runs after you, asking for a ride somewhere. Your roommate has a car, but you haven't seen it lately. You are in a hurry now, and your roommate has just asked for another ride.

_____

_____

_____

❖ 3.7 PERCEPTION CHECKING ❖

❖ **Activity Type: Oral Skill**

PURPOSE

To evaluate your skill at using perception-checking statements.

INSTRUCTIONS

1. Identify a situation in your life in which a perception check might be appropriate. Describe the situation to the person who will be evaluating your skill check.
2. Deliver a complete perception check to your evaluator, following the criteria listed on pages 115–116 of *Looking Out/Looking In* and outlined in the checklist below.
3. Describe
   a. how well perception checking might (or might not) work in the situation you have chosen. If you do not think a complete perception check is the best approach for this situation, explain why and describe a more promising alternative.
   b. the degree to which you could (or could not) increase your communicative competence by using perception checks in other situations.

CHECKLIST

5 = superior   4 = excellent   3 = good   2 = fair   1 = poor

_____   Describes background for potential perception-checking situation.

_____   Delivers complete perception check

      _____   Reports at least one behavior that describes what the person has said or done.

      _____   States two interpretations that are distinctly different, equally probable, and are based on the reported behavior.

      _____   Makes a sincere request for feedback clarifying how to interpret the reported behavior.

_____   Verbal and nonverbal behavior reflects sincere desire for clarification of the perception.

      _____   Uses language that accepts responsibility for the interpretation made.

      _____   Uses nonthreatening, nondefensive voice and eye contact.

_____   Realistically and clearly assesses how perception checking and other alternatives can be used in everyday life.

      _____   In situation described here.

      _____   In other situations.

✤ 3.8 PILLOW METHOD ✤
◆❖ Activity Type: Oral Skill

PURPOSE

To use the Pillow Method to illustrate understanding of multiple perspectives on a given issue.

INSTRUCTIONS

1. Use the material from *3.3 Shifting Perspectives (Pillow Method)* to share each position from the "Pillow Method" with either the real-life person involved in this issue or a classmate.
2. Invite your partner to correct you if you have misunderstood his or her position, or ask a classmate to role-play your partner, interrupting you if she or he thinks another aspect of the issue has been neglected. Use perception checking, as necessary, to clarify perceptions with your partner.
3. Based on your experience in this skill check, describe how you could integrate the Pillow Method into your relationships.

CHECKLIST

5 = superior   4 = excellent   3 = good   2 = fair   1 = poor

Engages in appropriate nonverbal behavior
     —looks at partner
     —speaks in nondefensive tone
     —faces partner

Presents relevant background information   _____

Explains Position 1 (I'm right; other person is wrong)   _____

Explains Position 2 (partner is correct/understandable)   _____

Explains Position 3 (both positions are correct/mistaken—even partly)   _____

Explains Position 4 (effects on relationship)   _____

Uses perception checking as necessary   _____

Presents conclusion   _____

Describes how Pillow Method could be applied to personal relationships   _____

                                 Total   _____

STUDY GUIDE

Check Your Understanding

MATCHING (KEY TERM REVIEW)

Match the terms in column 1 with their definitions in column 2.

_____ 1. androgynous

_____ 2. attribution

_____ 3. empathy

_____ 4. interaction constructs

_____ 5. membership constructs

_____ 6. perceptual schema

_____ 7. physical constructs

_____ 8. psychological constructs

_____ 9. punctuation

_____ 10. role constructs

_____ 11. self-serving bias

_____ 12. sympathy

_____ 13. perception checking

_____ 14. pillow method

_____ 15. omission

_____ 16. oversimplification

_____ 17. stereotyping

_____ 18. low-context

_____ 19. high-context

_____ 20. perspective-taking

a. compassion for another's situation
b. possessing both masculine and feminine traits
c. perceptual schema that categorize people according to their appearances
d. the process of determining the casual order of events
e. cognitive frameworks that allow individuals to organize perceptual data that they have selected from the environment
f. the tendency to interpret and explain information in a way that casts the perceiver in the most favorable manner
g. the ability to project oneself into another person's point of view, so as to experience the other's thoughts and feelings
h. the process of attaching meaning to behavior
i. perceptual schema that categorize people according to their social positions
j. perceptual schema that categorize people according to their social behaviors
k. perceptual schema that categorize people according to the groups to which they belong
l. perceptual schema that categorize people according to their apparent personalities
m. perceptual distortion in which some things are ignored
n. exaggerated generalizations associated with a categorizing system
o. a cultural language type using language clearly and logically
p. ability to take on the viewpoint of another person
q. an examination of the four sides and middle of a perceptual issue
r. perceptual distortion in which important information is left out
s. a cultural language type valuing social harmony over clarity
t. a quick tool for clarifying potential misunderstandings

Harcourt Brace & Company

TRUE/FALSE

Mark the statements below as true or false. Correct statements that are false on the lines below to create a true statement.

_____ 1. Since we are able to perceive with our senses, our perceptions make us aware of all that is going on around us.

_____

_____

_____ 2. Selection, organization, and interpretation comprise the three steps of the perception process.

_____

_____

_____ 3. The fact that we pay attention to some things and ignore others illustrates the fact that selection is an objective process.

_____

_____

_____ 4. Perceptual schema are cognitive frameworks that allow us to classify or organize the information we get about others.

_____

_____

_____ 5. It is wrong to generalize about anybody or any group, even if the generalizations are accurate.

_____

_____

_____ 6. We sometimes view people more favorably if we have a relationship with them.

_____

_____

_____ 7. Adrenal and sex hormones affect the way both men and women relate to each other.

_____

_____

Harcourt Brace & Company

_____ 8. All cultures view talk as desirable, using it for social purposes as well as to perform tasks.

_____

_____

_____ 9. Within the boundaries of a country, most perceptions are similar.

_____

_____

_____ 10. People with high self-esteem are more likely to think highly of themselves, and thus more likely to have a poor opinion of others.

_____

_____

COMPLETION

Fill in the blanks below with the correct terms chosen from the list below.

membership constructs	physical constructs	sympathy
interaction constructs	perceptual schema	empathy
psychological constructs	role constructs	stereotypes
androgynous		

1. _____ are the cognitive frameworks that allow individuals to organize perceptual data that they have selected from the environment.

There are five different ways that we organize these frameworks:

2. _____ are perceptual schema that categorize people according to their social position.

3. _____ are perceptual schema that categorize people according to their appearance.

4. _____ are perceptual schema that categorize people according to their apparent personalities.

5. _____ are perceptual schema that categorize people according to their social behavior.

6. _____ are perceptual schema that categorize people according to the groups to which they belong.

7. _____ is the ability to re-create another person's perspective.

Harcourt Brace & Company

8. _____ is feeling compassion for another person's predicament.

9. _____ are exaggerated beliefs associated with a categorizing system.

10. _____ is an example of a psychological sex type that influences perception.

MULTIPLE CHOICE

RECOGNIZING PERCEPTION-CHECKING ELEMENTS

For each of the following statements, identify which element of the perception-checking statement is missing. Place the letter of the most accurate evaluation of the statement on the line before the statement.

a. This statement doesn't describe behavior.
b. This statement doesn't give two distinctly different interpretations.
c. This statement neglects to request clarification of the perception.
d. There is nothing missing from this perception-checking statement.

_____ 1. "Why did you send me those flowers? Is this a special occasion or what?"

_____ 2. "When you went straight to bed when you came home, I thought you were sick. Are you all right?"

_____ 3. "You must be either really excited about your grades or anxious to talk about something important. What's going on?"

_____ 4. "When you ran out smiling, I figured you were glad to see me and ready to go, or maybe you were having such a good time here you wanted to stay longer."

_____ 5. "I thought you were angry with me when you didn't come over this afternoon like you'd said you would. But then I thought maybe something came up at work. What is it?"

_____ 6. "When you told me you expected to get an outline with my report, I thought you were trying to trick me into doing more work, or maybe you didn't realize that wasn't part of my job."

_____ 7. "When you told everyone my parents own the company, you must have been indicating I was hired here only because of them. Is that what you think?"

_____ 8. "When you passed the ball to me, I thought you wanted me to shoot. Did you?"

_____ 9. "Why is it that you're so pleased with yourself? Did you win the lottery or accomplish something great? What's up?"

_____ 10. "Dad, when you told my friend Art what a great athlete you think I am, I thought you were either really proud of me and wanted to brag a little, or maybe you wanted to see what Art and I had in common by the way he responded. What were you up to?"

Harcourt Brace & Company

CHAPTER 3 STUDY GUIDE ANSWERS

MATCHING (KEY TERM REVIEW)

1.	b	5.	k	9.	d	13.	t	17.	n
2.	h	6.	e	10.	i	14.	q	18.	o.
3.	g	7.	c	11.	f	15.	m	19.	s
4.	j	8.	l	12.	a	16.	r	20.	g

TRUE/FALSE

1.	F	3.	F	5.	F	7.	T	9.	F
2.	T	4.	T	6.	T	8.	F	10.	F

COMPLETION

1. perceptual schema
2. role constructs
3. physical constructs
4. psychological constructs
5. interaction constructs
6. membership constructs
7. empathy
8. sympathy
9. stereotypes
10. androgynous

MULTIPLE CHOICE

1.	b	3.	a	5.	d	7.	b	9.	a
2.	b	4.	c	6.	c	8.	b	10.	d

Harcourt Brace & Company

CHAPTER FOUR

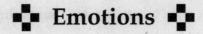

❖ Emotions ❖

OUTLINE

Use this outline to take notes as you read the chapter in the text and/or as your instructor lectures in class.

I. **COMPONENTS OF EMOTIONS**
   A. **Physiological Changes**
   B. **Nonverbal Reactions**
   C. **Cognitive Interpretations**

II. **TYPES OF EMOTIONS**
   A. **Primary and Mixed**
   B. **Intense and Mild**

III. **INFLUENCES ON EMOTIONAL EXPRESSION**
   A. **Culture**
   B. **Gender**
   C. **Social Conventions**
   D. **Social Roles**
   E. **Inability to Recognize Emotions**
   F. **Fear of Self-Disclosure**

IV. **GUIDELINES FOR EXPRESSING EMOTIONS**
   A. **Recognize Feelings**
   B. **Choose the Best Language**
      1. Single words
      2. What's happening to you
      3. What you'd like to do

Harcourt Brace & Company

C. Share Mixed Feelings

D. Recognize Difference Between Thinking and Acting

E. Accept Responsibility for Your Feelings

F. Choose the Best Time and Place to Express Your Feelings

G. Express Your Feelings Clearly
1. Avoid excessive length
2. Avoid overqualification or downplaying
3. Avoid "coded" feelings
4. Focus on a specific set of circumstances

V. MANAGING DIFFICULT EMOTIONS

A. Facilitative and Debilitative Emotions
1. Intensity
2. Duration

B. Thoughts Cause Feelings

C. Irrational Thinking and Debilitative Emotions
1. Fallacy of perfection
2. Fallacy of approval
3. Fallacy of shoulds
4. Fallacy of overgeneralization
    a. Limited amount of evidence
    b. Exaggerated shortcomings
    c. Abuse of the verb "to be"
5. Fallacy of causation
    a. Fail to have your own needs met
    b. Believe you cause emotions/pain for others
    c. Believe others cause your emotions
6. Fallacy of helplessness
7. Fallacy of catastrophic expectations

D. Minimizing Debilitative Emotions
1. Monitor your emotional reactions
2. Note the activating event
3. Record your self-talk
4. Dispute your irrational beliefs

KEY TERMS

Use these key terms to review major concepts from your text. Write the definition for each key term in the space to the right

activating event _____

cognitive interpretations _____

Harcourt Brace & Company

debilitative emotions _____

duration _____

emotional counterfeits _____

emotions _____

facilitative emotions _____

fallacy of approval _____

fallacy of catastrophic expectations _____

fallacy of causation _____

fallacy of helplessness _____

fallacy of overgeneralization _____

fallacy of perfection _____

fallacy of shoulds _____

intensity _____

irrational fallacies _____

mixed emotions _____

nonverbal reactions _____

overqualifying _____

physiological changes _____

Plutchik's "emotion wheel" _____

primary emotions _____

proprioceptive stimuli _____

rational–emotive therapy _____

self-talk _____

ACTIVITIES

✥ 4.1 THE COMPONENTS OF EMOTION ✥

❖ Activity Type: Skill Builder

PURPOSE

To help you identify the components of emotion.

INSTRUCTIONS

In groups, read each of the situations described below and describe how the emotions you would experience might manifest themselves in each of the components listed. Compare the responses of group members.

Harcourt Brace & Company

TABLE 4–A

Incident	Emotion(s)	Physiological Changes	Nonverbal Reactions	Cognitive Interpretation (Thoughts)
Example You've been assigned to deliver an oral presentation in one of your classes. It's now time to give your speech.	nervousness	pounding heart, churning stomach	quivery voice, slightly trembling hands	"I hope I don't make a fool of myself."
1. You're out on the town with friends for the evening. A companion asks you to dance.				
2. You're trying to study when a friend drops by, prepared to chat.				
3. You're telling a joke or story. Just as you reach the punch line, you notice your listener stifle a yawn.				
4. At the beginning of class, one of your professors says, "I'd like to talk to you in my office after the lecture."				

Harcourt Brace & Company

TABLE 4 – B

Incident	Emotion(s)	Physiological Changes	Nonverbal Reactions	Cognitive Interpretation (Thoughts)
5. An attractive friend whom you'd like to know better approaches you after an absence and gives you a hug, saying, "It's great to see you."				
6. You're discussing politics with a friend, who says, "I don't see how you can believe that!"				
7. A friend or relative has forgotten your birthday. She or he now apologizes.				
8. You overhear two preschool children pointing at you and saying, "Look at that silly!"				
9. Your romantic partner proposes marriage in front of friends. You're not ready.				
10. You are going in to your boss's office for your annual appraisal interview.				

Harcourt Brace & Company

❖ 4.2 FIND THE FEELINGS ❖

❖ **Activity Type: Skill Builder**

PURPOSES

1. To help you distinguish true feeling statements from counterfeit expressions of emotion.
2. To increase your ability to express your feelings clearly.

INSTRUCTIONS

1. In groups, identify the true feeling statements below.
2. Analyze the statements for accuracy of feeling (check your analysis at the end of this exercise).
3. Rewrite statements that do not clearly or accurately express the speaker's feelings. (HINT: Statements that could be prefaced with "I think" are not always expressions of emotions. If the statements could be preceded by "I am," there is a good likelihood that they express feelings.)

EXAMPLE

That's the most disgusting thing I've ever heard!

Analysis *This isn't a satisfactory statement, since the speaker isn't clearly claiming that he or she is* *disgusted.* _____

Restatement *I'm upset and angry that those parents left their young children alone overnight.* _____

1. That was a great evening!

   Analysis _____

   Restatement _____

   _____

2. You're being awfully sensitive about that.

   Analysis _____

   Restatement _____

   _____

3. I can't figure out how to approach him.

   Analysis _____

   Restatement _____

   _____

Harcourt Brace & Company

4. I'm confused about what you want from me.

Analysis _____

Restatement _____

_____

5. I love the way you've been so helpful.

Analysis _____

Restatement _____

6. I feel as if you're trying to hurt me.

Analysis _____

Restatement _____

_____

7. It's hopeless!

Analysis _____

Restatement _____

_____

8. I don't know how to tell you this . . .

Analysis _____

Restatement _____

_____

9. What's bothering you?

Analysis _____

Restatement _____

_____

10. I feel like the rug's been pulled out from under me.

Analysis _____

Restatement _____

_____

Harcourt Brace & Company

11. I feel like I've been stabbed in the back.

Analysis _____

Restatement _____

_____

12. You're so pathetic.

Analysis _____

Restatement _____

_____

ANSWERS TO "4.2 FIND THE FEELINGS"

1. This statement certainly implies some kind of positive feeling, but doesn't tell us clearly what it is.
2. The speaker here is labeling another's feelings, but saying nothing about his or her own. Is the speaker concerned, irritated, or indifferent to the other person's suspected sensitivity? We don't know.
3. The emotion here is implied but not stated. The speaker might be frustrated, perplexed, or tired.
4. Here is a clear statement of the speaker's emotional state.
5. We know the speaker loves the helpfulness, but does she or he love the helper or simply feel gratitude? Love is probably not an accurate description of the emotion, in any case.
6. Just because we say "I feel" doesn't mean a feeling is being expressed. This is an interpretation statement.
7. How does the speaker feel about the hopeless situation: resigned, sad, desperate? We haven't been told.
8. Again, no feeling stated. Is the speaker worried, afraid, distraught?
9. This could be a statement of concern, irritation, or genuine confusion. Nonverbal clues can help us decide, but a feeling statement would tell us for certain.
10. Here's a metaphorical statement of feeling, strongly suggesting surprise or shock. This sort of message probably does an adequate job of expressing the emotion here, but it might be too vague for some people to understand.
11. This is another metaphorical statement feeling, strongly suggesting hurt or betrayal. While this statement may do an adequate job of expressing the emotion, it might be misinterpreted by some people, and it might be too strong a statement for the actual situation.
12. This is the speaker's interpretation of someone else's behavior. It contains no feeling.

Harcourt Brace & Company

❖ 4.3 STATING EMOTIONS EFFECTIVELY ❖

❖ **Activity Type: Skill Builder**

PURPOSE

To help you express the emotions you experience clearly and appropriately.

INSTRUCTIONS

1. Identify what's ineffective or unclear about each of the following feeling statements.
2. Rewrite the feeling statements making them more effective. Use the following guidelines for sharing feelings:
   Recognize feelings
   Choose the best language
   Share mixed feelings
   Differentiate between feeling and acting
   Accept responsibility for your feelings
   Choose the best time and place to express
   Express your feelings clearly (concise, not overqualified, not coded, focused on specifics)

Feeling Statement	Identify Ineffective, Unclear Elements/Rewrite Statement
Example When you complimented me in front of everyone at the party, I was really embarrassed.	*I didn't express the mixed emotions I was feeling. I could have expressed this better by saying, "When you complimented me at the party, I was glad you were proud of me, but I was embarrassed that you did it in front of so many people."*
1. You make me so mad.	
2. I can't believe you act like that— I don't want to see you anymore.	
3. I don't care if you are rushed. We have to settle this now.	

Harcourt Brace & Company

Feeling Statement	Identify Ineffective, Unclear Elements/Rewrite Statement
4. I was a little ticked off when you didn't show up.	
5. You're always criticizing me.	
6. Sure would be nice if people expressed appreciation.	
7. You jerk—you forgot to put gas in the car.	
8. It's about time you paid up.	
9. You're the best! Thanks for everything!	
10. I feel like a heel.	
11. I guess I'm a little attracted to him.	
12. She sends me into outer space.	

❖ 4.4 SELF-TALK ❖

❖ Activity Type: Skill Builder

PURPOSES

1. To discover the self-talk in many common statements.
2. To identify any fallacies in self-talk.
3. To dispute any irrational self-talk.

INSTRUCTIONS

1. In groups, analyze the statements below.
2. Expand the self-talk behind each statement by using details from your personal experience to help discover things people think but often do not admit.
3. Identify any fallacies contained in the self-talk:

   approval   overgeneralization
   perfection   helplessness
   shoulds   catastrophic expectations
   causation

4. Dispute any irrational self-talk.

Statement	Self-talk	Fallacies	Dispute Any Fallacies
Example: He's too moody.	I can't stand his moodiness. He always acts depressed. I can never make him happy.	Overgeneralization, causation, and helplessness.	If I couldn't stand his moodiness, I would leave. He doesn't always act depressed. It is just that I get upset when I can't help him. It is not my responsibility to make him happy. I'll do what I can but not expect myself to solve all his problems.
1. I don't know why I even bother to study for her stupid tests.			

Statement	Self-talk	Fallacies	Dispute Any Fallacies
2. I never get any credit for trying around here.			
3. This place is unbearable with him around.			
4. He is so embarrassing because he has no manners.			
5. If I bring it up, we will fight.			
6. I hate him!			
7. I can't believe you told me to buy this stupid car!			

Statement	Self-talk	Fallacies	Dispute Any Fallacies
8. This guy is a total jerk.			
9. She's just like her mother.			
10. He's the perfect man. I'll be totally happy forever.			
11. I'll never get out of here because I can't make her stop talking.			
12. She thinks she's so gorgeous.			

Harcourt Brace & Company

As a group, identify the most common examples of your own self-talk, the fallacies involved, and the disputing you need to do to keep emotionally healthy.

Statement	Self-talk	Fallacies	Dispute Any Fallacies
1.			
2.			
3.			
4.			
5.			

Harcourt Brace & Company

✜ 4.5 DISPUTING IRRATIONAL THOUGHTS ✜

◆ Activity Type: Invitation to Insight

PURPOSE

To help you minimize debilitative emotions by eliminating irrational thinking.

INSTRUCTIONS

1. Use the chart opposite to record incidents in which you experience communication-related debilitative emotions. The incidents needn't involve overwhelming feelings: mildly debilitative emotions are appropriate for consideration as well.
2. For each incident (activating event), record the self-talk that leads to the emotion you experienced.
3. If the self-talk you've identified is based on any of the irrational fallacies described in *Looking Out/Looking In,* identify them.
4. In each case where irrational thinking exists, dispute the irrational fallacies and provide an alternative, more rational interpretation of the event.
5. Record your conclusions in the section at the end of this exercise.

Harcourt Brace & Company

Activating Event	Self-Talk	Based on Any Irrational Fallacies?	Emotion(s)	Dispute Irrational Thinking and Provide Alternative Interpretation
Example getting ready for job interview	"The employer will probably ask me a question I can't answer. I'll probably blow the interview. I'll never get a good job—it's hopeless!"	catastrophic failure overgeneralization helplessness	apprehension	There's certainly a *chance* that I'll blow the interview, but there's at least as good a chance that I'll do all right. I'm going overboard when I tell myself that there's no hope. The smartest idea is to do my best and not create a self-fulfilling prophecy of failing.
1.				
2.				
3.				
4.				
5.				

CONCLUSIONS

1. What are the situations in which you often experience debilitative emotions?

_____

_____

_____

_____

2. What irrational beliefs do you subscribe to most often? Label them and explain.

_____

_____

_____

_____

_____

3. How can you think more rationally to reduce the number and intensity of irrational emotions? (Give specific examples related to other aspects of your life, as well as referring to the activating events you have described in this exercise.)

_____

_____

_____

_____

_____

_____

_____

_____

_____

_____

Harcourt Brace & Company

STUDY GUIDE

CHECK YOUR UNDERSTANDING

MATCHING (KEY TERM REVIEW)

Match the terms in column 1 with their definitions in column 2.

_____ 1. debilitative emotions

_____ 2. facilitative emotions

_____ 3. mixed emotions

_____ 4. primary emotions

_____ 5. proprioceptive stimuli

_____ 6. self-talk

_____ 7. physiological change

_____ 8. nonverbal reactions

_____ 9. cognitive interpretations

_____ 10. Plutchik's emotion wheel

_____ 11. PONS test

_____ 12. emotional counterfeits

_____ 13. overqualifying

_____ 14. downplaying

_____ 15. intensity

_____ 16. duration

_____ 17. rational-emotive therapy

_____ 18. perfection fallacy

_____ 19. approval fallacy

_____ 20. catastrophic expectation fallacy

a. basic emotions
b. sensations activated by movement of internal tissues
c. the body's internal physical response to strong emotions
d. emotions that contribute to effective functioning
e. the nonvocal process of thinking
f. visible physical signs in response to strong emotions
g. thoughts accompanying strong emotions
h. emotions that prevent a person from functioning effectively
i. tool to measure the ability to recognize emotions expressed by others
j. emotions that are combinations of primary emotions
k. making a feeling statement stronger than it really is
l. tool for categorizing primary and mixed emotions
m. the strength of an emotion
n. making a feeling statement weaker than it really is
o. thinking or intending statements masquerading as feeling statements
p. belief about acceptance needed from others
q. the length of an emotion
r. belief about terrible consequences
s. cognitive approach to emotions saying that thoughts cause emotions
t. belief about communication performance

TRUE/FALSE

Mark the statements below as true or false. Correct statements that are false on the lines below to create a true statement.

_____ 1. According to Simbardo's survey of shyness, people who labeled themselves "not shy" behaved in virtually the same way as those people who labeled themselves "shy" in certain social situations.

_____

_____

_____ 2. Women consistently score higher than men on the PONS test, which measures the ability to recognize emotions that are expressed in the facial expressions, movements, and vocal cues of others.

_____

_____

_____ 3. In opposite-sex twosomes, research shows that the woman is almost always better at interpreting the man's nonverbal signals than the man is at interpreting the woman's.

_____

_____

_____ 4. In mainstream North American society, the unwritten rules of communication encourage the direct expression of most emotion.

_____

_____

_____ 5. "I feel confined" is an emotional counterfeit statement.

_____

_____

_____ 6. Using many words to express a feeling is better than just summarizing feelings in a few words.

_____

_____

Harcourt Brace & Company

_____ 7. A certain amount of negative emotion can be constructive or facilitative.

_____

_____

_____ 8. It's the interpretations people make of events that cause their feelings.

_____

_____

_____ 9. Subscribing to the myth of perfection may diminish your own self-esteem, but it won't keep others from liking you.

_____

_____

_____ 10. The rational-emotive approach to emotions is nothing more than trying to talk yourself out of feeling bad.

_____

_____

COMPLETION

Fill in the blanks below with the correct terms chosen from the list below.

catastrophic expectations	helplessness	causation
overgeneralization	shoulds	approval
perfection	activating event	monitoring
disputing		

1. _____ is an irrational fallacy that operates on the assumption that if something bad can possibly happen, it will.

2. _____ is an irrational fallacy that suggests that satisfaction in life is determined by forces beyond your control.

3. _____ is an irrational fallacy based on the belief that emotions are the result of other people and things rather than one's own self-talk.

4. _____ is an irrational fallacy that makes a broad claim based on a limited amount of evidence.

5. _____ is an irrational fallacy based on the inability to distinguish between what is and what ought to be.

6. _____ is an irrational fallacy in which people go to incredible lengths to seek acceptance from virtually everyone.

7. _____ is an irrational fallacy in which people believe that worthwhile communicators should be able to handle every situation with complete confidence and skill.

8. _____ is the single large incident or series of small incidents that lead to thoughts or beliefs about the incident.

9. _____ is the process of recognizing the physiological, nonverbal, and cognitive components of emotions.

10. _____ is the process of recognizing mistaken thinking and developing alternative thinking.

MULTIPLE CHOICE

Choose the letter of the irrational fallacy contained in the self-talk found below.

a. perfection
b. approval
c. shoulds
d. overgeneralization

e. causation
f. helplessness
g. catastrophic expectations

_____ 1. "If only I didn't put my foot in my mouth when I ask someone out."

_____ 2. "I just can't initiate conversations—that's all there is to it."

_____ 3. "He shouldn't be off with his friends on Friday night."

_____ 4. "If she doesn't like this shirt, I'll be so upset."

_____ 5. "There was a major fire the last time we left; there will probably be an earthquake this time."

_____ 6. "He's never romantic."

_____ 7. "She's a cold fish; I'm lucky if I get a kiss."

_____ 8. "You ought to drink less."

_____ 9. "You're going to die going to Mexico at spring break."

_____ 10. "I've had a class in interpersonal communication; I can't believe I insulted her just now."

_____ 11. "Shaw makes me so mad with all his great grades."

_____ 12. "She'll be devastated if I break up with her."

Harcourt Brace & Company

_____ 13. "It's not even worth trying to reach him."

_____ 14. "I hope they don't notice how much weight I've gained."

Choose the best answer for each of the statements below.

15. Which of the following statements about emotions and culture is true?

   a. The same events will generate the same emotions in all cultures.
   b. Certain basic emotions are experienced by all people around the world.
   c. People from different cultures express happiness and sadness with facial difference.
   d. Fear of strangers is as strong in Japan as it is in the U.S.

16. Which of the following statements about gender and emotion is true?

   a. Women and men are equally likely to express feelings of vulnerability.
   b. Men and women are equally good at recognizing the emotions of others.
   c. Men are less bashful about revealing their strengths and positive emotions than women are.
   d. The stereotypical female notion of emotional expressiveness is superior to that of the stereotypical male.

17. All of the following statements about social emotion are true _except:_

   a. Genuine emotional expressions are rare.
   b. The emotions that people do share directly are usually positive.
   c. Married couples disclose positive and negative feelings about absent third parties.
   d. Married couples disclose hostility feelings regularly.

18. Which of the following is a true feeling statement?

   a. "I feel like watching a movie."
   b. "I feel like you're lonely."
   c. "I'm irritated by the ticking clock."
   d. "I'm totally involved."

19. Which of the following _best_ improves the expression of emotion in the statement "I feel like giving up"?

   a. "I'm frustrated after asking him to pay his telephone bill three times."
   b. "I'm going to kill him."
   c. "I am going to tell the landlord about this frustrating situation."
   d. "I feel he's been unreasonable."

20. How could you improve your emotional expression in the statement "She makes me so totally upset, always thinking she is better than everyone else."

   a. take out the "totally."
   b. focus on a specific set of circumstances
   c. accept responsibility for your feelings
   d. All of the above could improve the statement.
   e. The statement is fine the way it is.

Harcourt Brace & Company

CHAPTER 4 STUDY GUIDE ANSWERS

MATCHING (KEY TERMS REVIEW)

1. h	5. b	9. g	13. k	17. s
2. d	6. e	10. l	14. n	18. t
3. j	7. c	11. i	15. m	19. p
4. a	8. f	12. o	16. q	20. r

TRUE/FALSE

1. T	3. F	5. F	7. T	9. F
2. T	4. F	6. F	8. T	10. T

COMPLETION

1. catastrophic expectations	5. shoulds	9. monitoring
2. helplessness	6. approval	10. disputing
3. causation	7. perfection	
4. overgeneralization	8. activating event	

MULTIPLE CHOICE

1. a	5. g	9. g	13. f	17. d
2. f	6. d	10. a	14. b	18. c
3. c	7. d	11. e	15. b	19. a
4. b	8. c	12. e	16. c	20. d

Harcourt Brace & Company

✥ Language: Barrier and Bridge ✥

OUTLINE

Use this outline to take notes as you read the chapter in the text and/or as your instructor lectures in class.

I. **THE NATURE OF LANGUAGE**
   A. **Language Is Symbolic**
   B. **Language Is Subjective**
   C. **Language Is Rule-Governed**
      1. Phonological rules
      2. Syntactic rules
      3. Semantic rules
      4. Pragmatic rules

II. **THE IMPACT OF LANGUAGE**
   A. **Naming and Identity**
   B. **Affiliation, Attraction, and Interest**
      1. Convergence
      2. Divergence
      3. Liking/interest
         a. Demonstrative pronoun choice
         b. Sequential placement
         c. Negation
         d. Duration
   C. **Power**

III. **USES (AND ABUSES) OF LANGUAGE**
   A. **Precision and Vagueness**
      1. Equivocation
      2. Abstraction
         a. High abstraction advantages
            1) Shorthand
            2) Avoid confusion

Harcourt Brace & Company

      b. High abstraction problems
          1) Stereotyping
          2) Confuse others
          3) Confuse yourself
          4) Lack of relational clarity
      c. Avoiding high-level abstractions with behavioral descriptions
          1) Who is involved?
          2) In what circumstances?
          3) What behaviors are involved?

B. The Language of Responsibility
    1. "It" statements
    2. "But" statements
    3. Questions
    4. "I" and "You" language
      a. "I" language
          1) Describes behavior
          2) Describes feelings
          3) Describes consequences
      b. Advantages of "I" language
          1) Defense reducing
          2) More honest
          3) More complete
      c. Problems with "I" language
          1) Anger interferes
          2) Other still gets defensive
          3) Sounds artificial
    5. "We" language

C. Disruptive Language
    1. Fact-opinion confusion
    2. Fact-inference confusion
    3. Emotive language

IV. GENDER AND LANGUAGE

A. Content

B. Reasons for Communicating

C. Conversational Style

D. Non-Gender Variables

E. Sex Roles—Social Orientation

V. CULTURE AND LANGUAGE

A. Verbal Communication Styles
    1. Low context/high context (level of directness)
    2. Elaborate/succinct
    3. Formal/informal

Harcourt Brace & Company

B. Language and Worldview
   1. Linguistic determinism
   2. Sapir-Whorf hypothesis
   3. Linguistic relativism

KEY TERMS

Use these key terms to review major concepts from your text. Write the definition for each key term in the space to the right

abstraction ladder _____

abstractions _____

behavioral description _____

CMM theory _____

convergence _____

disclaimers _____

elaborate _____

emotive language _____

equivocation _____

euphemisms _____

fact-inference confusion _____

fact-opinion confusion _____

formality _____

hedges _____

hesitations _____

high-context culture _____

"I" language _____

informality _____

intensifiers _____

Harcourt Brace & Company

language of power _____

language of responsibility _____

linguistic determinism _____

linguistic relativism _____

low-context culture _____

phonological rules _____

polite forms _____

powerless speech mannerisms _____

pragmatic rules _____

relative words _____

Sapir-Whorf hypothesis _____

semantic rules _____

sex roles _____

static evaluation _____

stereotyping _____

subscripting _____

succinct _____

syntactic rules _____

tag questions _____

"we" language _____

"you" language _____

Harcourt Brace & Company

ACTIVITIES

✛ 5.1 LABEL THE LANGUAGE ✛
❖ Activity Type: Skill Builder

PURPOSE

To help you recognize and change the imprecise language described in Chapter 5 of *Looking Out/Looking In*.

INSTRUCTIONS

1. In groups, label the language contained in each of the sentences below as relative language, emotive terms, or equivocal language.
2. Rewrite each sentence in more precise language.
3. Write your own examples of each variety of language in the space provided.
4. Compare your answers with those of the other groups.

EXAMPLE
I'm trying to diet, so give me a **small piece of cake.**
Language *Relative language* _____
Revised statement *I'm trying to diet, so give me a piece of cake about half the size of yours.* _____

1. I want to talk about **our relationship.**

   Language _____

   Revised statement _____

   _____

2. I'd like you to meet my **roommate** [of opposite sex].

   Language _____

   Revised statement _____

   _____

3. Helen is a **troublemaker.**

   Language _____

   Revised statement _____

   _____

Harcourt Brace & Company

4. Our candidate is trying to bring about a more **peaceful** world.

   Language _____

   Revised statement _____

   _____

5. We've known each other for a **long time**.

   Language _____

   Revised statement _____

   _____

6. Your essay should be **brief**.

   Language _____

   Revised statement _____

   _____

7. She's a very **mature** child for her age.

   Language _____

   Revised statement _____

   _____

8. Your contribution will help make government **more responsible to the people**.

   Language _____

   Revised statement _____

   _____

   _____

9. I don't understand **women** (or **men**)!

   Language _____

   Revised statement _____

   _____

Harcourt Brace & Company

10. He's a real **pest**.

   Language _____

   Revised statement _____

   _____

11. Stanley is an **ethical** person.

   Language _____

   Revised statement _____

   _____

12. We need to make some **changes** around here.

   Language _____

   Revised statement _____

   _____

13. I need **room to breathe**.

   Language _____

   Revised statement _____

   _____

14. Let's get her **something really nice**.

   Language _____

   Revised statement _____

   _____

15. He's **prejudiced**.

   Language _____

   Revised statement _____

   _____

16. Please leave **a brief message**.

Language _____

Revised statement _____

_____

17. You've got **really poor attendance**.

Language _____

Revised statement _____

_____

18. She is **too uptight**.

Language _____

Revised statement _____

_____

Now write your own examples of each type of language and revise the statements to illustrate alternative language.

1. Equivocal language _____

_____

Revised _____

_____

2. Relative language _____

_____

Revised _____

_____

3. Emotive language _____

_____

Revised _____

_____

Harcourt Brace & Company

❖ 5.2 BEHAVIORAL DESCRIPTIONS ❖

❖ Activity Type: Skill Builder

PURPOSE

To increase the clarity of your language by using behavioral descriptions.

INSTRUCTIONS

In each of the situations below, describe the behavior of an individual that might have led to the statement about him or her.

EXAMPLES
John's full of action.
John rode his bike for an hour and then mowed the lawn.
Meg is so much fun to be with.
Meg went shopping in the mall with me and laughed with me about how we looked in the new, looser styles.

1. That teacher is a bore!

   _____

   _____

2. That guy's real macho.

   _____

   _____

3. She's an all-around good person.

   _____

   _____

4. Mike's a hard worker.

   _____

   _____

5. Mark's real laid back.

   _____

   _____

6. Jill's such a dresser.

_____

_____

7. Josh is a real sport.

_____

_____

8. She gives me moral support.

_____

_____

9. Jack's motivated.

_____

_____

10. Peg is inspiring.

_____

_____

11. My parents are understanding.

_____

_____

12. Shelley's a flake!

_____

_____

13. You're too emotional.

_____

_____

14. He's so thoughtful.

_____

_____

❖ 5.3 LANGUAGE CLARITY ❖

❖ **Activity Type: Skill Builder**

PURPOSE

To increase the clarity of your language by revising phrases to describe an idea or act.

INSTRUCTIONS

For each of the statements below, write a clear description of the idea or act to clarify to your partner your intentions.

EXAMPLE
"Go over that way."
"Go across the footbridge, turn right, and go to the third building on your left."

1. Clean up your act.

   _____

   _____

2. This time, clean the car correctly.

   _____

   _____

3. Look more confident.

   _____

   _____

4. You add a bit of this and that and the sauce is finished.

   _____

   _____

5. This paper should be creative.

   _____

   _____

6. Make that report clearer.

_____

_____

7. Work harder on your studies.

_____

_____

8. Pay more attention.

_____

_____

9. Don't be so obnoxious!

_____

_____

10. Don't say things like that.

_____

_____

11. Clean up your room.

_____

_____

12. Be kind to your sister.

_____

_____

13. Get something good at the video store.

_____

_____

Harcourt Brace & Company

14. Fix a healthy dinner.

_____

_____

15. Show me that you care.

_____

_____

16. Your language is too pushy around my family.

_____

_____

17. You'll never get anywhere in the company talking like that.

_____

_____

18. You talk like a girl.

_____

_____

Harcourt Brace & Company

❖ 5.4 PRACTICING "I" LANGUAGE ❖

◆❖ Activity Type: Skill Builder

PURPOSE

To give you practice speaking descriptively, instead of evaluatively.

INSTRUCTIONS

Rewrite each of the evaluative "you" language statements below using descriptive "I" language.

EXAMPLE 1

"You don't care about my feelings."

"I felt hurt when I saw you in the restaurant with your old girlfriend. I'm worried that you might want to get back together with her."

EXAMPLE 2

"That was a dumb move!"

"Ever since you used the high setting to dry my favorite cotton shirt, it doesn't fit me anymore. That's why I'm so mad."

1. "Don't ever do that again."

   _____

   _____

   _____

2. "You're awfully sloppy."

   _____

   _____

   _____

3. "Why can't you be more reasonable?"

   _____

   _____

   _____

4. "All you do is talk about yourself."

_____

_____

_____

5. "I wish you'd try to be on time."

_____

_____

_____

6. "You're always taking but never giving."

_____

_____

_____

7. "You have no respect for my belongings!"

_____

_____

_____

8. "You don't listen to me."

_____

_____

_____

9. "Don't be so sensitive."

_____

_____

_____

10. "If you were a real friend, you wouldn't gossip about me."

_____

_____

_____

11. "Why don't you keep your promises?"

_____

_____

_____

12. "Why won't you be honest with me?"

_____

_____

_____

13. "You're unreliable."

_____

_____

_____

14. "You need to develop a little humility."

_____

_____

_____

15. "Why don't you just kick me while I'm down?"

_____

_____

_____

Harcourt Brace & Company

✚ 5.5 EXAMINING YOUR LANGUAGE ✚

◆ Activity Type: Invitation to Insight

PURPOSE

To help you analyze the types of language you use and the effectiveness of each.

INSTRUCTIONS

1. For each of the situations below, record the type of language used by the speaker. Evaluate its effectiveness. If you cannot identify with the situation, substitute one of your own.
2. Record the language you would use in response. Again, record your own situation and language if you have a relevant one.
3. Label the type of your language and its effectiveness. Focus on high and low abstraction, powerful or powerless speech mannerisms, facts or opinions, inferences, high- and low-context language styles and language and worldview.
4. Describe any alternative language you could use and its relative effectiveness.

EXAMPLE

Situation: Your supervisor at work has called you aside three times this week to correct work you have done. Each time she says, "You've messed up on this."

Type of language used with you/effectiveness: *My supervisor used "you" language and high abstraction. It wasn't very effective with me because I wasn't sure exactly what I'd messed up on, and I got very defensive, thinking she was about to fire me. She was very direct with me, however; she didn't keep silent about what was bothering her (this is consistent with the low-context culture in which I live).*

Language you'd use: *"You're on me all the time about something or other."*

Type of language and effectiveness: *"You" language and high abstraction. This is probably not very effective. My supervisor is likely to get defensive. Actually, my supervisor may think this is "helpful" and "caring" behavior and not realize that I am feeling hassled and threatened.*

Alternative language: *"Ms. Gomez, I'm worried that I'm not doing my job correctly because you've corrected me three times this week." This "I" language is more likely to let Ms. Gomez know what specifically is bothering me without raising a good deal of defensiveness. She's likely to appreciate my directness and specific request for help.*

1. Situation: You borrowed your friend's car and returned it with about 1 gallon of gas in it because you were too rushed to fill it. Now she says to you: "I'm perhaps just a little bit upset with you. That was rotten, don't you think?"

   Type of language used with you/effectiveness:

   _____

   _____

   Language you'd use:

   _____

   _____

Type of language and effectiveness:

_____

_____

Alternative language:

_____

_____

2. Situation: You have a hard time saying "no." Lately your roommate has been asking you to do chores that are not your responsibility. Tonight the roommate says, "You're such a great roommate. You won't mind doing the dishes for me tonight since I've got a date and you're just staying home anyway, will you?"

    Type of language used with you/effectiveness:

    _____

    _____

    Language you'd use:

    _____

    _____

    Type of language and effectiveness:

    _____

    _____

    Alternative language:

    _____

    _____

3. Situation: Cousins of yours are moving to town. They just called, addressing you by your old family nickname and said, "You lucky person, you get to have the pleasure of our company for a while until we find a place to live."

    Type of language used with you/effectiveness:

    _____

    _____

Harcourt Brace & Company

Language you'd use:

_____

_____

Type of language and effectiveness:

_____

_____

Alternative language:

_____

_____

4. Situation: You're working on a project with a partner from class, and the partner says, "We'll never get this done. You're too meticulous about everything."

    Type of language used with you/effectiveness:

    _____

    _____

    Language you'd use:

    _____

    _____

    Type of language and effectiveness:

    _____

    _____

    Alternative language:

    _____

    _____

Harcourt Brace & Company

5. Situation: Your boss's five-year-old is visiting the workplace. The child has broken two items and is now running from door to door, laughing loudly. Two customers look your way. Your boss says, "Chip off the old block, huh? Really an energetic kid!"

Type of language used with you/effectiveness:

_____

_____

Language you'd use:

_____

_____

Type of language and effectiveness:

_____

_____

Alternative language:

_____

_____

STUDY GUIDE

CHECK YOUR UNDERSTANDING

MATCHING (KEY TERM REVIEW)

Match the terms in column 1 with their definitions in column 2.

_____ 1. abstraction ladder

_____ 2. behavioral description

_____ 3. equivocal language

_____ 4. emotive language

_____ 5. euphemisms

_____ 6. high-context cultures

_____ 7. low-context cultures

_____ 8. "I" language

_____ 9. linguistic determinism

_____ 10. linguistic relativism

_____ 11. relative language

_____ 12. semantic rules

_____ 13. phonological rules

_____ 14. pragmatic rules

_____ 15. Sapir-Whorf hypothesis

_____ 16. static evaluation

_____ 17. stereotyping

_____ 18. syntactic rules

_____ 19. "you" language

_____ 20. sex role

a. ambiguous language that has two or more equally plausible meanings

b. cultures that avoid direct use of language, relying on the context of a message to convey meaning

c. an account that refers only to observable phenomena

d. cultures that use language primarily to express thoughts, feelings, and ideas as clearly and logically as possible

e. a statement that describes the speaker's reaction to another person's behavior without making judgments about its worth

f. a range of more to less abstract terms describing an event or object

g. language that conveys the sender's attitude rather than simply offering an objective description

h. pleasant terms substituted for blunt ones in order to soften the impact of unpleasant information

i. a moderate theory that argues that language exerts a strong influence on the perceptions of the people who speak it

j. govern what meaning language has, as opposed to what structure it has

k. the theory that a culture's worldview is unavoidably shaped and reflected by the language its members speak

l. govern how sounds are combined to form words

m. theory of linguistic determinism in which language is determined by a culture's perceived reality

n. language terms that gain their meaning by comparison

o. categorizing individuals according to a set of characteristics assumed to belong to all members of a group

p. govern what interpretation of a message is appropriate in a given context

q. govern the ways symbols can be arranged, as opposed to the meanings of those symbols

r. the social orientation that governs language behavior, rather than the biological gender

s. the tendency to view people or relationships as unchanging

t. a statement that expresses or implies a judgment of the other person

Harcourt Brace & Company

TRUE/FALSE

Mark the statements below as true or false. For statements that are false, correct them on the lines below to create a true statement.

_____ 1. Words are not arbitrary symbols; they have meaning in and of themselves.

_____

_____

_____ 2. According to research, your name is likely to affect people's first impressions of you.

_____

_____

_____ 3. Since research shows that people are rated as more competent when their talk is free of powerless speech mannerisms, it is obvious that a consistently powerful style of speaking is always the best approach.

_____

_____

_____ 4. Ambiguity and vagueness are forms of language that are to be avoided at all costs.

_____

_____

_____ 5. Ohio's Antioch College's sexual conduct code uses low-level abstractions to minimize the chances of anyone claiming confusion about a partner's willingness to engage in sexual behavior.

_____

_____

_____ 6. "How are we feeling today?" is an example of "we" language.

_____

_____

_____ 7. "Democrats are more responsive to the people than Republicans are" is an example of a fact statement.

_____

_____

_____ 8. According to research on language and gender, on the average, men discuss with men different topics than women discuss with other women.

_____

_____

_____ 9. Men are more likely to use language to accomplish the job at hand, while women are are more likely to use language to nourish relationships.

_____

_____

_____ 10. A person from the United States is more likely to value direct language than is someone from Japan.

_____

_____

COMPLETION

Fill in the blanks below with the correct terms chosen from the list below.

succinctness   equivocation   convergence   divergence   polite forms
tag questions   elaborateness   hedges   disclaimers   subscripting

1. _____ is the process of adapting one's speech style to match that of others with whom the communicator wants to identify.

2. _____ in language use involve denying direct responsibility for the statement, such as "I could be wrong, but . . . "

3. _____ of language involve using respectful terms of address, such as "You're welcome, ma'am."

4. _____ involves speaking in a way that emphasizes a person's differences from the other persons with whom he or she is speaking .

5. _____ in language use involves using words that more than one commonly accepted definition, such as "They eat _healthy_ food."

6. _____ in language use involve a negation statement, such as "_Didn't you think_ that party was boring?"

7. _____ in language use make less of the feeling or intention statement, such as "I'm _rather_ upset."

8. _____ in language use involves dating to reduce static evaluation, such as "Kanako$_{July\ 13}$ is nervous."

Harcourt Brace & Company

9. _____ involves speaking with few words, and it is usually most extreme in cultures where silence is valued.

10. _____ involves speaking with rich and expressive terms, sometimes involving strong assertions and exaggerations.

MULTIPLE CHOICE

Label the examples of language given below by writing the letter of the language type illustrated on the line in front of the example.

a. inference
b. relative word
c. euphemism
d. emotive word
e. equivocal language

_____ 1. John didn't call **so he must be angry**.

_____ 2. I have a **stomach problem**.

_____ 3. That place is **expensive**.

_____ 4. That guy is a real **hunk**.

_____ 5. I'd like **recognition** for my work.

_____ 6. The bathroom **needs some air**.

_____ 7. We need to make **progress** tonight.

_____ 8. The funeral director pointed out the **slumber room**.

_____ 9. He showed up, **so he must agree**.

_____ 10. That's a real **smart trick you pulled**.

_____ 11. My brother is a **sanitation engineer**.

_____ 12. Ian gave a **long** speech.

_____ 13. My grandfather is **young**.

_____ 14. My sister is a **pill**.

Choose the letter of the *least* abstract alternative to the high abstraction terms.

_____ 15. Jo's **constantly complaining**.

  a. Jo whines a lot.
  b. Jo complains often about the workload.
  c. Jo told me three times this week that she feels overworked.
  d. Every time we meet, Jo complains about all the work she does.

Harcourt Brace & Company

_____ 16. He can **never** do **anything** because he's **always busy**.

    a. He couldn't take me to the dinner because he had to work.
    b. He can never do anything fun because he's always working.
    c. He didn't ever take time off to be with me.
    d. He works too much so we have a boring life.

_____ 17. There are **a lot of problems** associated with **freedom**.

    a. Freedom carries with it responsibility.
    b. Since I moved into my own apartment, I have to pay ten bills.
    c. I don't like all the responsibility of living on my own.
    d. My economic responsibilities limit my freedom.

_____ 18. Shannon is **worthless** as a roommate.

    a. Shannon is always gone, so she's really not part of our house.
    b. Shannon never does her part around here.
    c. Shannon's jobs seldom get done around here.
    d. Shannon has attended only one of our six house meetings.

_____ 19. Carlos is the **most wonderful friend**.

    a. Carlos has never told anyone about my fear of failing.
    b. Carlos listens to me about everything.
    c. Carlos is the best listener I've ever met.
    d. I can trust Carlos implicitly with all my secrets.

_____ 20. Keiko **goes overboard** in trying to make people like her.

    a. Keiko gave everyone on the team a valentine.
    b. Keiko is the biggest kiss-up you ever met.
    c. I think Keiko is trying to make my friends like her better than me.
    d. I want Keiko to stop trying to outdo everybody else.

Harcourt Brace & Company

CHAPTER 5 STUDY GUIDE ANSWERS

MATCHING (KEY TERM REVIEW)

1.	f	5.	h	9.	k	13.	l	17.	o
2.	c	6.	b	10.	i	14.	p	18.	q
3.	a	7.	d	11.	n	15.	m	19.	t
4.	g	8.	e	12.	j	16.	s	20.	r

TRUE/FALSE

1.	F	3.	F	5.	T	7.	F	9.	T
2.	T	4.	F	6.	F	8.	T	10.	T

COMPLETION

1. convergence
2. disclaimers
3. polite forms
4. divergence
5. equivocation
6. tag questions
7. hedges
8. subscripting
9. succinctness
10. elaborateness

MULTIPLE CHOICE

1.	a	5.	e	9.	a	13.	b	17.	b
2.	c	6.	c	10.	d	14.	d	18.	d
3.	b	7.	e	11.	c	15.	c	19.	a
4.	d	8.	c	12.	b	16.	a	20.	a

Harcourt Brace & Company

✙ Nonverbal Communication: Messages without Words ✙

OUTLINE

Use this outline to take notes as you read the chapter in the text and/or as your instructor lectures in class.

I. **NONVERBAL COMMUNICATION**
   A. **Social Importance**
      1. Mehrabian: 93 percent
      2. Birdwhistle: 65 percent
   B. **Definition: Those Messages Expressed by Other Than Linguistic Means**

II. **CHARACTERISTICS OF NONVERBAL COMMUNICATION**
   A. **Nonverbal Communication Exists**
   B. **Nonverbal Behavior Has Communicative Value**
      1. Deliberate
      2. Unintentional
   C. **Nonverbal Communication Is Culture-Bound**
   D. **Nonverbal Communication Is Primarily Relational**
      1. Identity management
      2. Definition of relationships we want with others
      3. Conveyance of emotion
   E. **Nonverbal Communication Serves Many Functions**
      1. Repeating
      2. Substituting
      3. Complementing
      4. Accenting
      5. Regulating
      6. Contradicting
   F. **Nonverbal Communication Is Ambiguous**

III. DIFFERENCES BETWEEN VERBAL AND NONVERBAL COMMUNICATION

A. Single versus Multiple Channels

B. Discrete versus Continuous

C. Clear versus Ambiguous

D. Verbal versus Nonverbal Impact

E. Deliberate versus Unconscious

IV. TYPES OF NONVERBAL COMMUNICATION

A. Body Orientation

B. Posture
   1. Forward/backward lean
   2. Tension/relaxation

C. Gestures
   1. Preening behaviors
   2. Manipulators

D. Face and Eyes
   1. Complexity
   2. Speed
   3. Emotions reflected
   4. Microexpression
   5. Kinds of messages
      a. Involvement
      b. Positive/negative attitude
      c. Dominance/submission
      d. Interest (pupils)

E. Voice (Paralanguage): Tone, Speed, Pitch, Number and Length of Pauses, Volume, Disfluencies

F. Touch

G. Physical Attractiveness

H. Clothing

I. Proxemics (Space)
   1. Intimate
   2. Personal
   3. Social
   4. Public

J. Territoriality

K. Physical Environment

L. Time (Chronemics)

Harcourt Brace & Company

KEY TERMS

Use these key terms to review major concepts from your text. Write the definition for each key term in the space to the right.

accenting _____

affect blends _____

ambiguous messages _____

body orientation _____

chronemics _____

complementing _____

congruence _____

convergence _____

contradicting _____

deception cues _____

disfluencies _____

double messages _____

emblems _____

gestures _____

identity management _____

illustrators _____

intimate distance _____

kinesics _____

leakage _____

manipulators _____

microexpression _____

nonverbal communication _____

Harcourt Brace & Company

paralanguage _____

personal distance _____

posture _____

preening behavior _____

proxemics _____

public distance _____

regulating _____

relaxation cue _____

repeating _____

social distance _____

substituting _____

tension cue _____

territory _____

touch _____

Harcourt Brace & Company

ACTIVITIES

❖ 6.1 DESCRIBING NONVERBAL STATES ❖

❖ **Activity Type: Skill Builder**

PURPOSE

To describe the nonverbal behaviors that indicate various emotional and attitudinal states.

INSTRUCTIONS

NOTE: Group members (or individuals) may want to make videotaped examples of their own behavior reflecting each of the situations below or they may want to collect television or movie examples illustrating the emotions and attitudes described below.

1. For each of the statements below, record the nonverbal behaviors that reflect the attitude or emotions described.
2. Compare your responses with those of others in the class and note the similarities and differences in your responses.

Statement	Nonverbal Behavior
Example She listens well.	Turns body toward me, leans forward, smiles once or twice, nods, maintains eye contact about 80 percent of the time.
1. He acts so cool.	
2. She's a tease.	
3. He's paranoid.	

Statement	Nonverbal Behavior
4. She's flirting. (Use Table 6.2 from the text if you need help here.)	
5. He's stressing out.	
6. She takes over.	
7. He's overdramatic.	
8. She acts confidently.	
9. He seems friendly.	
10. She's "hyper."	

COMPARISONS

Record the similarities and differences you found when comparing your responses to those of your classmates.

_____

_____

_____

_____

Harcourt Brace & Company

❖ 6.2 NONVERBAL COMPLAINTS ❖

❖ Activity Type: Skill Builder

PURPOSE

To facilitate the display of nonverbally congruent behaviors.

INSTRUCTIONS

For each statement below, describe the nonverbal behaviors that might satisfy the person making the complaints. Compare your advice with that of others in the class, noting the differences different people or contexts may have on the advice.

Complaint	Nonverbal Advice
Example He says I'm too eager to please.	Take a little more time to respond after a request. Lean toward the person a little less. Smile, but don't keep the smile on your face continuously. Gesture, but don't gesture as quickly. Stand a little more erect and hold all the parts of your body more still.
1. She says I'm too serious.	
2. My boss says not to be so aggressive.	
3. He says I could be more helpful.	
4. Friend or relative says I don't really care about him or her.	
5. I sound stupid when I hear myself on tape.	

Complaint	Nonverbal Advice
6. They look so sure of themselves, but I just can't act that way.	
7. I'd like to look more relaxed.	
8. I don't want them to think I'm indifferent.	
9. She says I act too cold.	
10. He says I should be more open.	

Compare your advice with that of others in the class. Note any similarities or differences.

_____

_____

_____

_____

How might the persons involved or the context change the advice you would give?

_____

_____

_____

_____

_____

Harcourt Brace & Company

❖ 6.3 NONVERBAL HOW-TO'S ❖

❖ Activity Type: Skill Builder

PURPOSE

To define what you and others in the class consider effective nonverbal behavior in some social situations.

INSTRUCTIONS

1. For each of the social situations below, list the nonverbal behaviors you believe will achieve the stated goal.
2. Compare your answers with those of others in your class.
3. Reflect on the behavior of yourself and others important to you. How might you change some of the nonverbal cues you display to communicate what you desire more effectively?

Social Situations	Nonverbal Behaviors
Example Initiate conversation with a stranger at a party.	Make eye contact, offer hand in greeting, smile, come within four feet of other person, turn body toward other person, nod occasionally when other is talking.
1. Take control or exercise leadership in a class group.	
2. Come across well in a job interview.	
3. Tell an interesting joke or story.	
4. Appear friendly and warm.	

Social Situations	Nonverbal Behaviors
5. Signal your desire to leave a conversation when the other person keeps on talking.	
6. Appear confident when asking boss for a raise.	
7. Appear interested in class lecture.	
8. Avoid talking with an undesirable person.	
9. Let a friend know you need to leave.	
10. Appear concerned about a friend's dilemma.	

Compare your answers with others in class. Note the areas of agreement and disagreement.

_____

_____

_____

_____

_____

_____

Are there situations or contexts in which the described behaviors could be changed to appear more effective?

_____

_____

_____

_____

_____

If you could ask someone close to you to change his or her nonverbal behavior in a certain situation, what would you ask him or her to change and how would you tell him or her to communicate more effectively nonverbally?

_____

_____

_____

_____

_____

Harcourt Brace & Company

❖ 6.4 CONGRUENT MESSAGES ❖
◆ Activity Type: Invitation to Insight

PURPOSE

1. To analyze the verbal and nonverbal aspects of your communication behaviors.
2. To weigh the consequences of sending congruent versus incongruent messages.

INSTRUCTIONS

1. In each of the following situations, describe your likely verbal and nonverbal behaviors necessary to make the situation *congruent*. Use descriptions of the eleven types of nonverbal communication described in Chapter 6 of *Looking Out/Looking In* (e.g., body orientation, posture, gesture, face and eyes, voice, touch, physical attractiveness, clothing, proxemics, territoriality, physical environment, and time).
2. Describe four situations from your own life and how you would send verbal and nonverbal messages that are congruent or incongruent. Include a brief discussion of the consequences of your congruent or incongruent behaviors.
3. Answer the questions about congruency at the end of this exercise.

Situation	Your Verbal Behavior	Your Nonverbal Behavior	How Congruent Are the Verbal/Nonverbal Messages?	Possible Consequences of This Congruency/Incongruency
Example Person I like a lot takes me out to dinner and I have a good time and enjoy the food.	"I'm really enjoying this; the food is terrific and so is the company."	I look at my partner when I talk, smiling and tilting my head slightly forward. I lean toward my partner and touch my partner lightly on the arm and hand.	My verbal and nonverbal behaviors are very congruent in this context.	I hope the consequences are that my partner will understand how much I care and enjoy our time together. I run the risk of not "game playing," of course—in that I could be hurt if my partner's feelings don't match mine, but I think the chances are pretty slim in this instance.
1. My boss calls me into the office to tell me what a good job I've been doing lately.				
2. My roommate has dinner ready when I get home after a rough day.				
3. My relative drops in to visit me when other people are over for the evening.				
4. My lab partner suggests that we go out partying together Friday night.				
5. My friend asks to borrow my favorite sweater.				

Situation of Your Own	Your Optimal Verbal Behavior	Your Optimal Nonverbal Behavior	Congruency/Incongruency
1.			
2.			
3.			
4.			

Harcourt Brace & Company

Consider situations in addition to the examples in this exercise when answering the following questions.

In what situations is it wise, and when is it unwise, to express your emotions "congruently"?

_____

_____

_____

_____

_____

Describe situations in which congruity is desirable. Describe how you could best match your verbal and nonverbal behaviors in these situations.

_____

_____

_____

_____

_____

_____

_____

Harcourt Brace & Company

STUDY GUIDE

CHECK YOUR UNDERSTANDING

MATCHING (KEY TERM REVIEW)

Match the terms in column 1 with their definitions in column 2.

_____ 1. accenting

_____ 2. chronemics

_____ 3. complementing

_____ 4. contradicting

_____ 5. deception cues

_____ 6. disfluency

_____ 7. double message

_____ 8. emblems

_____ 9. illustrators

_____ 10. kinesics

_____ 11. leakage

_____ 12. manipulators

_____ 13. microexpressions

_____ 14. nonverbal communication

_____ 15. paralanguage

_____ 16. posture

_____ 17. proxemics

_____ 18. regulating

_____ 19. repeating

_____ 20. substituting

a. nonverbal behavior that reinforces a verbal message

b. a nonlinguistic verbalization: *um, er, ah* and the like

c. nonverbal behaviors that reveal information a communicator does not disclose verbally

d. brief facial expressions

e. nonverbal behavior that emphasizes part of a verbal message

f. contradiction between a verbal message and one or more nonverbal cues

g. messages expressed by other than linguistic means

h. the study of how people and animals use space

i. the study of how humans use and structure time

j. nonverbal behavior that is inconsistent with a verbal message

k. the way in which individuals carry themselves: erect, slumping, and so on

l. nonverbal behavior that controls the flow of verbal messages in a conversation

m. nonverbal behavior that takes the place of a verbal message

n. nonverbal behavior that signals the untruthfulness of a verbal message

o. deliberate nonverbal behaviors with precise meanings, known to virtually all members of a cultural group

p. nonlinguistic means of vocal expression: rate, pitch, tone, and so on

q. nonverbal behavior that duplicates the content of a verbal message

r. movements in which one part of the body grooms, massages, rubs, holds, fidgets, pinches, picks or otherwise manipulates another part

s. the study of body position and motion

t. nonverbal behaviors that accompany and support verbal messages

Harcourt Brace & Company

TRUE/FALSE

Mark the statements below as true or false. Correct statements that are false on the lines below to create a true statement.

_____ 1. Nonverbal behaviors are, by their nature, intentional.

_____

_____

_____ 2. Certain nonverbal behaviors like smiling are universal, and thus they are used exactly the same around the world.

_____

_____

_____ 3. The concept of nonverbal convergence illustrates that skilled communicators can adapt their behavior when interacting with members of other cultures or subcultures in order to make the exchange more smooth and effective.

_____

_____

_____ 4. Nonverbal communication is much better suited to expressing attitudes and feelings than it is to expressing ideas.

_____

_____

_____ 5. Research on nonverbal communication and lying shows that individuals who are trying to deceive others are more likely to show nonverbal evidence of lying if they haven't had a chance to rehearse their lying and when they feel strongly about the information being hidden.

_____

_____

_____ 6. In studies of detecting lying, men are consistently more accurate than women at detecting the lies and discovering the underlying truth.

_____

_____

_____ 7. Both verbal and nonverbal messages are communicated one at a time, rather like pearls on a string.

_____

_____

_____ 8. Unlike verbal communication that is discrete (has a clear beginning and end), nonverbal communication is continuous and never ending.

_____

_____

_____ 9. The nonverbal impact of messages is more powerful than the verbal impact.

_____

_____

_____ 10. Nonverbal communication is clearer than verbal communication.

_____

_____

COMPLETION

Fill in the blanks below with the correct terms chosen from the list below.

intimate	personal	social	public	relaxation
paralanguage	preening	affect blend	touch	body orientation

1. _____ is the distance zone identified by Hall that ranges from four to about twelve feet; within it are the kinds of communication that usually occur in business.

2. _____ is a postural cue such as leaning back or lowering shoulders that a higher status person usually exhibits when not feeling threatened.

3. _____ behaviors, such as stroking or combing one's hair (whether they are conscious or unconscious), signal an interest in another individual.

4. _____ is the distance zone identified by Hall that ranges from eighteen inches to four feet and includes behavior found in most social conversations.

5. _____ is the combination of two or more expressions in different parts of the face.

6. _____ is the degree to which we face toward or away from someone with our body, feet, and head.

Harcourt Brace & Company

7. _____ is the distance zone identified by Hall that ranges from skin contact to about eighteen inches; we usually use this distance with people in private who are emotionally very close to us.

8. _____ is the distance zone identified by Hall that ranges from twelve feet outward and includes communication such as that found in a typical classroom.

9. _____ is nonverbal behavior that includes having a foreign accent.

10. _____ is nonverbal behavior that includes brushing up against someone.

MULTIPLE CHOICE

Choose the letter of the type of nonverbal communication that is illustrated below.

a. environment   b. paralinguistics   c. proxemics   d. territoriality

_____ 1. No one dared to sit in Ralph's chair.

_____ 2. Jeremy put a "NO ENTRANCE" sign on his door.

_____ 3. The students rearranged the chairs in the classroom.

_____ 4. Manuela stepped back three feet from her friend.

_____ 5. The lovers were sitting only inches apart.

_____ 6. Rob's voice softened when he spoke to her.

_____ 7. There was a long pause after the decision was made.

_____ 8. Mitchell sighed audibly.

_____ 9. Gretchen took the third seat down from Yayoi.

_____ 10. Kevin was annoyed that someone was leaning on his car.

a. body orientation   b. gesture   c. touch   d. face and eyes

_____ 11. The children playfully kicked one another.

_____ 12. Professor Jimenez illustrated her lecture with many arm movements.

_____ 13. Leland shifted his shoulders toward the speaker.

_____ 14. Ernie avoided looking at her.

_____ 15. The executive stared at her employee.

_____ 16. Martin turned his body away from his brother.

_____ 17. The officer pointed in the correct direction.

_____ 18. Letoya didn't appreciate the slap on the back.

_____ 19. Blake set his jaw in disgust.

_____ 20. Francesca signaled "OK" across the room.

Harcourt Brace & Company

CHAPTER 6 STUDY GUIDE ANSWERS

MATCHING (KEY TERM REVIEW)

1.	e	5.	n	9.	t	13.	d	17.	h
2.	i	6.	b	10.	s	14.	g	18.	l
3.	a	7.	f	11.	c	15.	p	19.	q
4.	j	8.	o	12.	r	16.	k	20.	m

TRUE/FALSE

1.	F	3.	T	5.	T	7.	F	9.	T
2.	F	4.	T	6.	F	8.	T	10.	F

COMPLETION

1. social
2. relaxation
3. preening
4. personal
5. affect blend
6. body orientation
7. intimate
8. public
9. paralanguage
10. touch

MULTIPLE CHOICE

1.	d	5.	c	9.	c	13.	a	17.	b
2.	d	6.	b	10.	d	14.	d	18.	c
3.	a	7.	b	11.	c	15.	d	19.	d
4.	c	8.	b	12.	b	16.	a	20.	b

❖ Listening: More Than Meets the Ear ❖

OUTLINE

Use this outline to take notes as you read the chapter in the text or as your instructor lectures in class.

I. **LISTENING IS IMPORTANT**

II. **ELEMENTS IN THE LISTENING PROCESS**
   A. **Hearing**
   B. **Attending**
   C. **Understanding**
   D. **Responding**
   E. **Remembering**

III. **TYPES OF NONLISTENING**
   A. **Pseudolistening**
   B. **Stage Hogging**
   C. **Selective Listening**
   D. **Insulated Listening**
   E. **Defensive Listening**
   F. **Ambushing**
   G. **Insensitive Listening**

IV. **WHY WE DON'T LISTEN**
   A. **Message Overload**
   B. **Preoccupation**
   C. **Rapid Thought**
   D. **Effort**

E. External Noise

F. Hearing Problems

G. Faulty Assumptions
   1. Heard it all before
   2. Speaker's words too simple
   3. Speaker's words too complex
   4. Subject is uninteresting

H. Lack of Apparent Advantages
   1. Control
   2. Admiration/respect
   3. Energy release

I. Lack of Training

V. INFORMATIONAL LISTENING

A. Talk Less

B. Get Rid of Distractions

C. Don't Judge Prematurely

D. Look for Key Ideas

E. Questions
   1. Ask sincere questions
      a. clarify thoughts and feelings
      b. underused
         1) people are reluctant to ask
         2) people think they already understand
   2. Avoid counterfeit questions
      a. trap the speaker
      b. make statements
      c. carry hidden agendas
      d. seek "correct" answers
      e. based on unchecked assumptions

F. Paraphrase

VI. LISTENING TO HELP

A. Advising
   1. Be correct
   2. Be sure other is ready to accept
   3. Best if blame is not likely

B. Judging
   1. Asked for judgment
   2. Constructive judgment

C. **Analyzing**
1. Be tentative
2. Have chance of being correct
3. Receptive other
4. Motivated to be helpful

D. **Questioning**
1. Don't ask to satisfy your own curiosity
2. Don't confuse or distract
3. Don't disguise suggestions/criticism

E. **Supporting**
1. Types
   a. agreement
   b. offers to help
   c. praise
   d. reassurance
   e. diversion
2. Potential problems
   a. Deny others the right to their feelings
   b. minimize the situation
   c. focus on "then and there"
   d. cast judgment
   e. defend yourself
   f. rain on the speaker's parade
3. Guidelines
   a. Approval not necessary
   b. Monitor reaction

F. **Prompting**

G. **Paraphrasing**
1. Thoughts
2. Emotions
3. When to use paraphrasing
   a. If the problem is complex enough
   b. If you have necessary time and concern
   c. If you are genuinely interested in helping
   d. If you can withhold judgment
   e. If you're comfortable with style and don't overuse it

H. **Which Style to Use?**
1. Consider the situation
2. Consider the other person
3. Consider yourself

KEY TERMS

Use these key terms to review major concepts from your text. Write the definition for each key term in the space to the right.

active listening _____

advising _____

ambushing _____

analyzing _____

attending _____

conversational narcissist _____

counterfeit questions _____

defensive listening _____

elements in listening process _____

hearing _____

insensitive listening _____

insulated listening _____

judging _____

paraphrasing _____

parroting _____

prompting _____

pseudolistening _____

questioning response _____

residual message _____

responding _____

selective listening _____

shift-response _____

sincere questions _____

stage hogging _____

supporting _____

understanding _____

verbatim _____

Harcourt Brace & Company

ACTIVITIES

❖ 7.1 LISTENING DIARY ❖
◆ Activity Type: Invitation to Insight

PURPOSES

1. To help you identify the styles of listening you use in your interpersonal relationships.
2. To help you discover the consequences of the listening styles you use.

BACKGROUND

Looking Out/Looking In identifies several styles of listening and nonlistening that you can use when seeking information from another:

pseudolistening	insensitive listening
stage hogging	ambushing
selective listening	prompting
insulated listening	questioning
defensive listening	paraphrasing

INSTRUCTIONS

1. Use the following form to record the listening styles you use in various situations.
2. After completing your diary, record your conclusions in the space provided.

Time and Place	People	Subject	Listening Style(s)	Consequences
Example Saturday night party	my date and several new acquaintances	good backpacking trips	*stage hogging:* I used everybody's remarks to show what a hotshot explorer I am.	I guess I was trying to get everyone to like me. My egotistical attitude probably accomplished the opposite!
1.				
2.				
3.				

CONCLUSIONS

Based on your observations here, what styles of listening and nonlistening do you use most often? In what situations do you use each of these styles? (Consider the people involved, the time, subject, and your personal mood when determining situational variables.)

_____

_____

_____

_____

_____

_____

_____

What are the consequences of the listening styles you have just described?

_____

_____

_____

_____

_____

_____

_____

❖❖ 7.2 RESPONSES TO PROBLEMS ❖❖

❖ **Activity Type: Skill Builder**

PURPOSE

To help you practice the various styles of responding to others' problems.

INSTRUCTIONS

For each of the problem statements below, write a response in each style of helping discussed in *Looking Out/Looking In*. Make your response as realistic as possible.

EXAMPLE

"I don't know what to do. I tried to explain to my professor why the assignment was late, but he wouldn't even listen to me."

Advising *You ought to write him a note. He might be more open if he has time to read it and think about it.*

Judging *You have to accept these things. Moping won't do any good, so quit feeling sorry for yourself.*

Analyzing *I think the reason he wasn't sympathetic is because he hears lots of excuses this time of year.*

Supporting *All of your work has been so good that I'm sure this one assignment won't matter. Don't worry!*

Questioning *What did he say? Do you think he'll change his mind later? How could you make up the assignment?*

Prompting *(Short silence) And so . . . ?*

Paraphrasing *You sound really discouraged, since he didn't even seem to care about your reasons—is that it?*

1. My girlfriend says she wants to date other guys this summer while I'm out in the boondocks working on construction. She claims it's just to keep busy and that it won't make any difference with us, but I think she wants to break off permanently, and she's trying to do it gently.

   Advising _____

   _____

   Judging _____

   _____

   Analyzing _____

   _____

   Supporting _____

   _____

Harcourt Brace & Company

Questioning _____

_____

Prompting _____

_____

Paraphrasing _____

_____

2. My roommate and I can't seem to get along. She's always having her boyfriend over, and he doesn't know when to go home. I don't want to move out, but I can't put up with this much longer. If I bring it up I know my roommate will get defensive, though.

Advising _____

_____

Judging _____

_____

Analyzing _____

_____

Supporting _____

_____

Questioning _____

_____

Prompting _____

_____

Paraphrasing _____

_____

3. What do you do about a friend who borrows things and doesn't return them?

Advising _____

_____

Judging _____

_____

Analyzing _____

_____

Supporting _____

_____

Questioning _____

_____

Prompting _____

_____

Paraphrasing _____

4. The pressure of going to school and doing all the other things in my life is really getting to me. I can't go on like this, but I don't know where I can cut back.

Advising _____

_____

Judging _____

_____

Analyzing _____

_____

Supporting _____

_____

Questioning _____

_____

Prompting _____

_____

Paraphrasing _____

_____

Harcourt Brace & Company

5. You think that by the time you become an adult your parents would stop treating you like a child, but not mine! If I wanted their advice about how to live my life, I'd ask.

Advising _____

_____

Judging _____

_____

Analyzing _____

_____

Supporting _____

_____

Questioning _____

_____

Prompting _____

_____

Paraphrasing _____

_____

❖ 7.3 PARAPHRASING PRACTICE ❖

❖ Activity Type: Skill Builder

PURPOSE

To develop your ability to paraphrase in order to gain information about another person's thoughts.

INSTRUCTIONS

Write a paraphrasing response for each of the following statements. Include the speaker's thoughts and, as appropriate, the speaker's feelings.

EXAMPLE

"It's not fair that I have to work so much. Other students can get better grades because they have the time to study."
So your job is taking time away from your studies and you think you're at a disadvantage?

1. "I guess it's OK for you to use my computer. Just be careful to handle the floppy disks only by the cover, and don't put any food or drinks on the desk or anywhere near the machine. This computer cost me a lot of money, and it would be a disaster if anything happened to it."

    _____

    _____

    _____

2. "You'll have the best chance at getting a loan for the new car you want if you give us a complete financial statement and credit history."

    _____

    _____

    _____

3. (Instructor to student) "This paper shows a lot of promise. It could probably earn you an A grade if you just develop the idea about the problems that arise from poor listening a bit more."

    _____

    _____

    _____

4. "I do like the communication course, but it's not at all what I expected. It's much more *personal*, if you know what I mean."

_____

_____

_____

5. "We just got started on your car's transmission. I'm pretty sure we can have it ready tonight."

_____

_____

_____

6. "I do think it's wrong to take any lives, but sometimes I think certain criminals deserve capital punishment."

_____

_____

_____

7. "We are planning to have some friends over tonight, but I guess you're welcome to come too. Why don't you just bring along something we can munch on so we'll be sure to have enough food?"

_____

_____

_____

8. "You know I enjoy spending time with you. But I have other friends, too!"

_____

_____

_____

❖ 7.4 LISTENING FOR FEELINGS ❖

❖ Activity Type: Skill Builder

PURPOSE

To help you identify the feelings that are often implied but not stated by others.

INSTRUCTIONS

For each of the statements below, write the feeling or feelings that the speaker might be experiencing.

Possible Feeling(s)	Speaker's Remarks
Example puzzlement, hurt	It seems like you haven't been paying much attention to me lately. Is there something wrong?
1.	1. I wonder if I ought to start looking for another job. They're reorganizing the company, and what with a drop in business and all, maybe this is one of the jobs they'll cut back on. But if my boss finds out I'm looking around, maybe he'll think I don't like it here and let me go anyway.
2.	2. It was a great game. I played a lot, I guess, but I only scored once. The coach put Ryan in ahead of me.
3.	3. I said I'd do the collecting for him, but I sure don't feel like it. But I owe him a favor, so I guess I'll have to do it.
4.	4. I've got a report due tomorrow, an exam the next day, rehearsals every night this week, and now a meeting this afternoon. I don't think I can even fit in eating, and this has been going on all month.
5.	5. Sure she gets better grades than I do. She's a housewife, takes only two classes, and all she has to do is study. I have to work a job and go to school, too. And I don't have anyone to support me.
6.	6. I can't understand why they haven't written. They've never been gone this long without at least a card, and I don't even know how to get in touch with them.

Possible Feeling(s)	Speaker's Remarks
7.	7. We had a great evening last night. The dinner was fantastic; so was the party. We saw lots of people; Erin loves that sort of thing.
8.	8. My daughter got straight A's this year, and the high school has a reputation for being very hard. She's a natural student. But sometimes I wonder if she isn't all books. I wish I could help her get interested in something besides studying.
9.	9. Boy, the teacher tells us he'll mark off on our grade every time we're late, but it doesn't seem to bother him when he comes in late. He must figure it's his privilege.
10.	10. I worked up that whole study—did all the surveying, the compiling, the writing. It was my idea in the first place. But he turned it in to the head office with his name on it, and he got the credit.
11.	11. I don't know whether I'm doing a good job or not. She never tells me if I'm doing well or need to work harder. I sure hope she likes my work.
12.	12. She believed everything he said about me. She wouldn't even listen to my side, just started yelling at me.
13.	13. Look, we've gone over and over this. The meeting could have been over an hour ago if we hadn't gotten hung up on this one point. If we can't make a decision, let's table it and move on.
14.	14. Look, I know I acted like a rat. I apologized, and I'm trying to make up for it. I can't do any more, can I? So drop it!
15.	15. How can I tell him how I really feel? He might get mad and then we'd start arguing. He'll think I don't love him if I tell him my real feelings.

Harcourt Brace & Company

❖ 7.5 PROBLEM-SOLVING PARAPHRASING ❖

◆❖ Activity Type: Skill Builder

PURPOSE

To help you become skillful at giving paraphrasing responses to others' problems.

BACKGROUND

You have already learned that the most helpful paraphrasing responses reflect both the speaker's thoughts and feelings. In order for this style of helping to be effective, you also have to sound like yourself, and not another person or a robot. There are many ways to reflect another's thoughts and feelings:

> "It sounds like you're . . ."
> "I hear you saying . . ."
> "Let me see if I've got it. You're saying . . ."
> "So you're telling me . . ."

INSTRUCTIONS

Write a paraphrasing response for each of the statements that follow. Be sure that the response fits your style of speaking, while at the same time it reflects the speaker's *thoughts* and *feelings*.

EXAMPLE

"Stan always wants to tell me about the women he's going out with; he gives me `blow-by-blow' descriptions of their dates that take hours, and he never seems to ask about who I'm going out with or what I'm interested in."

"It seems like you might be tired (feeling) of hearing about Stan's love life (thoughts) and maybe a little put-out (feeling) that he doesn't solicit information from you about whom you're dating (thoughts)— is that it?"

1. "I can't believe it! First the instructor said my answers were too skimpy, so I gave her more information. Now she tells me I'm being too wordy. Arggh!"

   _____

   _____

   _____

2. "What would you do if you heard your best friend making fun of you behind your back?"

   _____

   _____

   _____

Harcourt Brace & Company

3. "We can't decide whether to put Grandmother in a nursing home. She hates the idea, but she can't take care of herself anymore, and it's just too much for us."

_____

_____

_____

4. "Those damn finals are finally over. I'm never going to even *think* about history again!"

_____

_____

5. "I'm really starting to hate my job. Every day I do the same boring, mindless work. But if I quit, I might not find any better work."

_____

_____

_____

6. "They haven't called me in ages. I think they must be mad at me or something."

_____

_____

_____

7. "Maybe I'll just use their lawn as a bathroom. Then they'll understand what their dog is doing to my yard!"

_____

_____

_____

8. "Why don't you try to be a little less messy around here? This place looks like a dump!"

_____

_____

_____

❖ 7.6 PARAPHRASING INFORMATION ❖

❖ Activity Type: Skill Builder

INSTRUCTIONS

1. Join with three partners to create a foursome. Label the members A, B, C, and D.
2. A and B review the list below, choosing the topic upon which they disagree most widely.
3. A and B conduct a five-minute conversation on the topic they have chosen. During this period, the speakers may not express their own ideas until they have paraphrased the other person's position to his or her satisfaction. (If A and B finish discussing one item, they should move on to a second one from the list below.)
   C observes A   D observes B
4. At the end of the conversation, the observers should review the listening with the persons they observed.
5. Steps 1–5 are now repeated with the roles of conversationalists and observers reversed.

TOPICS

Indicate your position on each statement below by circling one of the following labels:

TA = totally agree   A = agree   D = disagree   TD = totally disagree

1. Despite the value of classes like this one, in the last analysis good communicators are born, not made.	TA	A	D	TD
2. One measure of a person's effectiveness as a communicator is how well he or she is liked by others.	TA	A	D	TD
3. No matter how unreasonable or rude they are, people deserve to be treated with respect.	TA	A	D	TD
4. An effective communicator should be able to handle any situation in a way that leaves the other person feeling positive about the interaction.	TA	A	D	TD
5. Interpersonal communication classes should be a required part of everyone's college education.	TA	A	D	TD
6. Most of what is taught in interpersonal communication classes is really common sense.	TA	A	D	TD

OR as an alternative

1. Choose a topic of interest to you and a partner (music, politics, religion, men, women, morals, etc.). It is best if you anticipate some difference of opinion on the topic.
2. Take turns stating your opinion. The only rule is that before you can take your turn stating *your* opinion, you must paraphrase the content of your partner's opinion *to his or her satisfaction.*

Harcourt Brace & Company

❖ 7.7 LISTENING EFFECTIVENESS ❖

❖ **Activity Type: Oral Skill**

PURPOSE

To give you practice in using different listening styles to enhance listening effectiveness.

INSTRUCTIONS

1. With a partner, decide on communication situations that require effective listening. The situations should be real for the person describing them and might involve a problem, a decision that needs to be made, an issue of importance, or a change in a relationship.
2. Have your partner tell you the problem/issue/decision/relationship while you listen effectively.
3. You then tell your partner of your problem/issue/decision/relationship while your partner listens effectively.
4. Analyze the listening styles you used. Which were most/least effective in this situation? Which styles do you need to work on?
5. Use the checklist below to evaluate listening effectiveness.

CHECKLIST

5 = superior   4 = excellent   3 = good   2 = fair   1 = poor

Uses appropriate nonverbal attending behaviors   _____
    faces the speaker
    sits upright or leans slightly toward speaker
    looks in direction of speaker
    facial expression indicates interest
    vocal tone reflects interest

Uses a balance of the following types of listening responses, as appropriate   _____
    nonleading questions
    prompting
    analyzing
    advising
    supporting
    paraphrasing
        reflects speaker's *thoughts*
        reflects speaker's *feelings*
        remains tentative, inviting feedback from speaker
        Based on self-observation (class feedback, videotape, etc.)
        and personal reflection analyzes   _____
Which listening styles were most/least effective in this situation?
Which listening styles need to be worked on?

                                              Total   _____

Harcourt Brace & Company

STUDY GUIDE

CHECK YOUR UNDERSTANDING

MATCHING (KEY TERM REVIEW)

Match the terms in column 1 with their definitions in column 2.

_____ 1. active listening

_____ 2. advising

_____ 3. ambushing

_____ 4. analyzing

_____ 5. attending

_____ 6. defensive listening

_____ 7. hearing

_____ 8. insensitive listening

_____ 9. insulated listening

_____ 10. judging

_____ 11. paraphrasing

_____ 12. prompting

_____ 13. pseudolistening

_____ 14. questioning

_____ 15. responding

_____ 16. selective listening

_____ 17. stage-hogging

_____ 18. supporting

_____ 19. understanding

_____ 20. verbatim

a. a helping style in which the listener offers an interpretation of a speaker's message

b. the physiological dimensions of listening

c. a response style in which the receiver ignores undesirable information

d. a helping response in which the receiver offers suggestions about how the speaker should deal with a problem

e. restating a speaker's thoughts and feelings in the listener's own words

f. a style in which the receiver listens carefully in order to gather information to use in an attack on the speaker

g. a reaction in which the receiver evaluates the sender's message either favorably or unfavorably

h. using silences and brief statements of encouragement to draw out a speaker

i. the process of filtering out some messages and focusing on others

j. a style of helping in which the receiver seeks additional information from the sender (sometimes disguised advice)

k. a response style in which the receiver responds only to messages that interest him or her

l. a response style in which the receiver perceives a speaker's comments as an attack

m. accepting the speaker's words at face value, resulting in failure to recognize the thoughts or feelings that are not directly expressed by a speaker

n. a listening style in which the receiver is more concerned with making his or her own point than in understanding the speaker

o. occurs when sense is made of a message

p. a response in which the words of the speaker are repeated

q. a response style in which the receiver reassures, comforts, or distracts the person seeking help

r. giving observable feedback to the speaker

s. an imitation of true listening in which the receiver's mind is elsewhere

t. restating a speaker's thoughts and feelings in the listener's own words

Harcourt Brace & Company

TRUE/FALSE

Mark the statements below as true or false. Correct statements that are false on the lines below to create a true statement.

_____ 1. We spend more time listening to others than in any other type of communication.

_____

_____

_____ 2. Speaking is active; listening is passive.

_____

_____

_____ 3. All interruptions are attempts at stage-hogging.

_____

_____

_____ 4. Given the onslaught of messages to listen to every day, it is understandable (and perhaps even justifiable) to use pseudolistening and other nonlistening responses.

_____

_____

_____ 5. In careful listening, the heart rate quickens and respiration increases.

_____

_____

_____ 6. People speak at about the same rate as others are capable of understanding their speech.

_____

_____

_____ 7. The advantages of listening are more obvious to people than the advantages of speaking.

_____

_____

_____ 8. Paraphrasing is the most accurate listening response you can make.

_____

_____

_____ 9. Judging listening responses may be favorable or negative.

_____

_____

_____ 10. Even an accurate form of analytic listening can create defensiveness since it may imply superiority and evaluativeness.

_____

_____

COMPLETION

Fill in the blanks below with the correct terms chosen from the list below.

residual message   shift-response   conversational narcissist
sincere question   counterfeit question   constructive criticism
agreement   praise   reassurance
diversion

1. _____ is a name given to a nonlistening stage-hog.

2. _____ is a genuine request for new information aimed at understanding others.

3. _____ is the information we store (remember) after processing information from teachers, friends, radio, TV, and other sources.

4. _____ is a type of state-hogging strategy in which the focus of the conversation is changed from the speaker to the stage-hog.

5. _____ is a query that is a disguised attempt to send a message, not receive one.

6. _____ is a lesser form of negative judgment which is intended to help the problem-holder improve in the future.

7. _____ is a listening response that helps speakers by getting their minds off their troubles and on to something else.

8. _____ is a listening response that supports others by telling them how wonderful they are.

Harcourt Brace & Company

9. _____ is a listening response that encourages others to go on despite the problems of the immediate situation.

10. _____ is a listening response designed to show solidarity with speakers by telling them how right they are.

MULTIPLE CHOICE

Match the letter of the listening type with its example found below.

a. advising   c. analyzing   e. supporting   g. paraphrasing
b. judging   d. questioning   f. prompting

_____ 1. "So what do you mean?"

_____ 2. "You're mad at me for postponing the meeting?"

_____ 3. "You're probably just more upset than usual because of the stress of exams."

_____ 4. "What reason did she give for not attending?"

_____ 5. "Well, that was good of him not to complain."

_____ 6. "Have you tried praising her?"

_____ 7. "Have you tried talking to him about it?"

_____ 8. "Are you as excited as you sound about this big meet?"

_____ 9. "Jim should not have said that to Amy after you asked him not to."

_____ 10. "And then what happened?"

_____ 11. "So why did you go to Ellie's in the first place?"

_____ 12. "You really are good; they'll recognize that."

_____ 13. "It's not fair for you to have to work nights."

_____ 14. "Maybe you should give her a taste of her own medicine."

_____ 15. "And so you feel like retaliating because you're hurt?"

_____ 16. "Maybe you're a little insecure because of the divorce?"

_____ 17. "Like what?"

_____ 18. "What makes you think that he's cheating?"

_____ 19. "You've always pulled out those grades before—I know you can do it again."

_____ 20. "She's probably jealous so that's why she's doing that."

Choose the best informational paraphrasing response to each statement below.

21. Boss to employee: "Draft a letter that denies this request for a refund, but make it tactful."

    a. "What do you want me to say?"
    b. "How can I say no tactfully?"
    c. "So I should explain nicely why we can't give a refund, right?"
    d. "In other words, you want me to give this customer the brush-off?"

22. Friend says, "How do they expect us to satisfy the course requirements when there aren't enough spaces in the classes we're supposed to take?"

    a. "So you're frustrated because you can't get into the courses you need, huh?"
    b. "You think that some of the courses are worthless—is that it?"
    c. "Sounds like you're sorry you chose this major."
    d. "Why don't you write a letter to the chairperson of the department?"

23. Friend says, "Why don't I meet you after class at the student union?"

    a. "So you want me to pick you up at the student union?"
    b. "You want me to pick you up *again*?"
    c. "So we'll meet at the south entrance around 5:15?"
    d. "Why can't you drive yourself? Is your car broken again?"

24. Co-worker advises, "When you go in for a job interview, be sure and talk about the internship, your coursework, and your extracurricular activities. Don't expect them to ask you."

    a. "You think they won't ask about those things?"
    b. "Won't that sound like bragging?"
    c. "Why should I talk about the internship?"
    d. "So you're saying not to be bashful about stressing my experience?"

25. Friend says, "I don't think it's right that they go out and recruit women when there are plenty of good men around."

    a. "Sounds like you're angry because you think they're so concerned about being fair to women that they're being unfair to men, right?"
    b. "You're right—that doesn't sound fair."
    c. "If you don't think it's fair, you ought to speak up."
    d. "I can see that you're angry. What makes you think women are being given an unfair advantage?"

For each of the statements below, identify which response is the most complete and accurate problem-solving reflection of the speaker's thoughts and feelings.

26. "Sometimes I think I'd like to drop out of school, but then I start to feel like a quitter."

    a. "Maybe it would be helpful to take a break. You can always come back, you know."
    b. "You're afraid that you might fail if you stay in school now, is that it?"
    c. "I can really relate to what you're saying. I feel awkward here myself sometimes."
    d. "So you'd feel ashamed of yourself if you quit now, even though you'd like to?"

Harcourt Brace & Company

27. "I don't want to go to the party. I won't know anyone there, and I'll wind up sitting by myself all night."

    a. "You're afraid that you won't be able to approach anybody and nobody will want to talk to you?"
    b. "You never know; you could have a great time."
    c. "So you really don't want to go, eh?"
    d. "What makes you think it will be that way?"

28. "I get really nervous talking to my professor. I keep thinking that I sound stupid."

    a. "Talking to her is really a frightening experience?"
    b. "You're saying that you'd rather not approach her?"
    c. "You get the idea that she's evaluating you, and that leaves you feeling uncomfortable?"
    d. "You think that talking to her might affect your grade for the worse?"

29. "I don't know what to do about my kids. Their whining is driving me crazy."

    a. "Even though whining is natural, it's getting to you?"
    b. "Sometimes you really get fed up with their complaining?"
    c. "You're getting angry at them?"
    d. "Even the best parents get irritated sometimes."

30. "I just blew another test in that class. Why can't I do better?"

    a. "You probably need to study harder. You'll get it!"
    b. "You're feeling sorry for yourself because you've done all you can do and you still can't pull a better grade?"
    c. "Where do you think the problem is?"
    d. "You're discouraged and frustrated because you don't know what you're doing wrong?"

Harcourt Brace & Company

CHAPTER 7 STUDY GUIDE ANSWERS

MATCHING (KEY TERM REVIEW)

1. e	5. i	9. c	13. s	17. n
2. d	6. l	10. g	14. j	18. q
3. f	7. b	11. t	15. r	19. o
4. a	8. m	12. h	16. k	20. p

TRUE/FALSE

1. T	3. F	5. T	7. F	9. T
2. T	4. T	6. F	8. F	10. T

COMPLETION

1. conversational narcissist
2. sincere question
3. residual message
4. shift-response
5. counterfeit question
6. constructive criticism
7. diversion
8. praise
9. reassurance
10. agreement

MULTIPLE CHOICE

1. f	7. a	13. b	19. e	25. a
2. g	8. g	14. a	20. c	26. d
3. c	9. b	15. g	21. c	27. a
4. d	10. f	16. c	22. a	28. c
5. b	11. d	17. f	23. c	29. b
6. a	12. e	18. d	24. d	30. d

Harcourt Brace & Company

CHAPTER EIGHT

❖ Intimacy and Distance in Relationships ❖

OUTLINE

Use this outline to take notes as you read the chapter in the text or as your instructor lectures in class.

I. **INTIMACY AND DISTANCE IN RELATIONSHIPS**
   A. **Intimacy and Distance: Striking a Balance**
   B. **Dimensions of Intimacy**
      1. Physical
      2. Intellectual
      3. Emotional
      4. Shared activities
   C. **Male and Female Intimacy Styles**
      1. Self-disclosure
      2. Shared activities
   D. **Cultural Influences on Intimacy**
      1. Historical
      2. Cultural
         a. Class
         b. Individualist
         c. Collectivist

II. **PRELUDE TO INTIMACY: INTERPERSONAL ATTRACTION**
   A. **We Like People Who Are Similar to Us—Usually**
   B. **We Like People Who Are Different from Us—In Certain Ways**
   C. **We Like People Who Like Us—Usually**
   D. **We Are Attracted to People Who Can Help Us**
   E. **We Like Competent People—Particularly When They're Human**
   F. **We Are Attracted to People Who Disclose Themselves to Us—Appropriately**
   G. **We Feel Strongly About People We Encounter Often**

III. DEVELOPMENTAL STAGES IN INTIMATE RELATIONSHIPS

A. Stages of Relational Communication
1. Initiating
2. Experimenting
3. Intensifying
4. Integrating
5. Bonding
6. Differentiating
7. Circumscribing
8. Stagnating
9. Avoiding
10. Terminating

B. Characteristics of Relational Development and Maintenance
1. Not all relationships move through all ten steps
2. Intimacy is not the only goal of relationships
3. Movement occurs within stages
4. Movement between steps is generally sequential
5. Relationships are constantly changing
   a. Connection and autonomy
   b. Openness and privacy
   c. Predictability and novelty
6. Movement is always to a new place

IV. SELF-DISCLOSURE IN RELATIONSHIPS

A. Definition
1. Deliberate
2. Significant
3. Not known by others

B. Degrees of Self-Disclosure
1. Social penetration model: Breadth and depth
2. Levels: Clichés, facts, opinions, feelings

C. A Model of Self-Disclosure: Open, Hidden, Blind, Unknown

D. Characteristics of Self-Disclosure
1. Usually occurs in dyads
2. Occurs incrementally
3. Few transactions involve high levels
4. Relatively scarce
5. Usually occurs in positive relationships

E. Reasons for Self-Disclosure
1. Catharsis
2. Self-clarification
3. Self-validation
4. Reciprocity
5. Impression formation
6. Relationship maintenance and enhancement
7. Social control
8. Manipulation

Harcourt Brace & Company

V. ALTERNATIVES TO SELF-DISCLOSURE

    A. Lies

        1. White lies

        2. Reasons for lying

            a. Save face

            b. Avoid tension/conflict

            c. Guide social interaction

            d. Expand/reduce relationships

            e. Gain power

        3. Effects of lies

    B. Equivocation

    C. Hinting

    D. The Ethics of Evasion

VI. GUIDELINES FOR SELF-DISCLOSURE

    A. Consider the Importance of the Other Person

    B. Evaluate the Risks Involved

    C. Make the Amount and Type of Self-Disclosure Appropriate

    D. Make the Disclosure Relevant to the Situation at Hand

    E. Reciprocate Disclosure as Appropriate

    F. Consider Constructive Effects

    G. Make the Disclosure Clear and Understandable

KEY TERMS

Use these key terms to review major concepts from your text. Write the definition for each key term in the space to the right.

attraction variables _____

avoiding _____

bonding _____

breadth _____

catharsis _____

circumscribing _____

clichés _____

depth _____

Harcourt Brace & Company

dialectical tension _____

differentiating _____

emotional intimacy _____

equivocal language _____

exchange theory _____

experimenting _____

facts _____

feelings _____

hinting _____

impression formation _____

initiating _____

integrating _____

intellectual intimacy _____

intensifying _____

intimacy _____

Johari Window _____

lie _____

manipulation _____

opinions _____

physical intimacy _____

reciprocity _____

relational enhancement _____

self-clarification _____

self-disclosure _____

self-validation _____

Harcourt Brace & Company

small talk _____

social control _____

social penetration _____

stages of relationships _____

stagnating _____

terminating _____

uncertainty reduction _____

white lie _____

Harcourt Brace & Company

ACTIVITIES

❖ 8.1 ATTRACTION VARIABLES ❖

◆ **Activity Type: Invitation to Insight**

PURPOSE

To identify the attraction variables that led to your relationship with two persons important to you.

INSTRUCTIONS

1. Identify two people who are not blood relatives with whom you have important relationships. Briefly describe the relationship of Person A and Person B below.
2. Comment on each of the attraction variables listed below for each relationship. Describe how that variable did or did not play a role in the development of your relationship.

Attraction Variable	Person A Relationship	Person B Relationship
1. We are similar to one another.		
2. We are different from one another—in complementary ways.		
3. We like one another.		
4. We help one another.		
5. We view one another as competent but human.		

Harcourt Brace & Company

Attraction Variable	Person A Relationship	Person B Relationship
6. We engage in appropriate self-disclosure.		
7. We see one another frequently.		

Summarize the ways in which you are attracted to others. What types of relationships require what types of attraction as far as you are concerned? Describe the differences in attraction for romantic relationships versus friendships or professional relationships.

_____

_____

_____

_____

_____

_____

Harcourt Brace & Company

❖ 8.2 BREADTH AND DEPTH OF RELATIONSHIPS ❖

◆ Activity Type: Invitation to Insight

PURPOSES

1. To help you understand the breadth and depth of a relationship that is important to you.
2. To help you decide if you are satisfied with the breadth and depth of that relationship, and possibly to modify it.

INSTRUCTIONS

1. Use the form below to make a social penetration model for a significant relationship you have, indicating the depth and breadth of various areas. See Figure 8.4 and 8.5 in Chapter 8 of *Looking Out/Looking In* for an example of the social penetration model.
2. Answer the questions at the end of the exercise.

SOCIAL PENETRATION MODEL

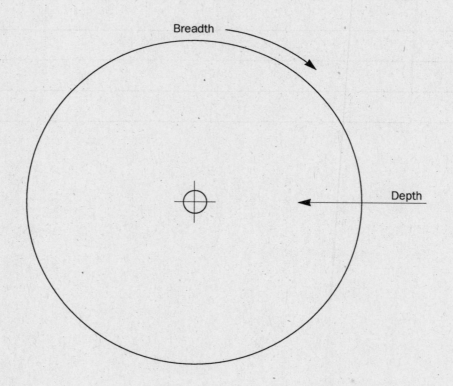

Significant relationship described:

CONCLUSIONS

How deep or shallow is your relationship with this person?

_____

_____

Does the depth vary from one area (breadth) to another? In what way?

_____

_____

_____

Are you satisfied with the depth and breadth of this relationship?

_____

_____

_____

What could you do to change the relationship?

_____

_____

_____

_____

_____

_____

_____

_____

_____

Harcourt Brace & Company

✜ 8.3 REASONS FOR NONDISCLOSURE* ✜

◆ Activity Type: Invitation to Insight

PURPOSE

To give you an idea of the reasons you do not disclose and the rationality of these reasons.

INSTRUCTIONS

1. Choose a particular individual about whom you want to analyze your self-disclosing behavior.
2. In the column to the left of each item, indicate the extent to which you use each reason to avoid disclosing.

   5 = almost always   2 = rarely
   4 = often   1 = never
   3 = sometimes

3. In the column to the right of each item, indicate how reasonable and realistic the reason is.

   5 = totally realistic
   4 = mostly realistic
   3 = partly realistic, partly unrealistic
   2 = mostly unrealistic
   1 = totally unrealistic

How Frequently Do You Use the Reason?		How Realistic and Rational Is the Reason?
_____	1. I can't find the opportunity to self-disclose with this person.	_____
_____	2. If I disclose I might hurt the other person.	_____
_____	3. If I disclose I might be evaluating or judging the person.	_____
_____	4. I can't think of topics that I would disclose.	_____
_____	5. Self-disclosure would give information that might be used against me at some time.	_____
_____	6. If I disclose it might cause me to make personal changes.	_____
_____	7. Self-disclosure might threaten relationships I have with people other than the close acquaintance to whom I disclose.	_____
_____	8. Self-disclosure is a sign of weakness.	_____
_____	9. If I disclose I might lose control over the other person.	_____
_____	10. If I disclose I might discover I am less than I wish to be.	_____

*Based on a survey developed by Lawrence B. Rosenfeld, "Self-Disclosure Avoidance: Why Am I Afraid to Tell You Who I Am?" *Communication Monographs* 46 (1979): 63–74.

**How Frequently
Do You Use
the Reason?**

**How Realistic
and Rational
Is the Reason?**

_____ 11. If I disclose I might project an image I do not want to project. _____

_____ 12. If I disclose the other person might not understand what
I was saying. _____

_____ 13. If I disclose the other person might evaluate me negatively. _____

_____ 14. Self-disclosure is a sign of some emotional disturbance. _____

_____ 15. Self-disclosure might hurt our relationship. _____

_____ 16. I am afraid that self-disclosure might lead to an intimate
relationship with the other person. _____

_____ 17. Self-disclosure might threaten my physical safety. _____

_____ 18. If I disclose I might give information that makes me
appear inconsistent. _____

_____ 19. Any other reasons: _____ _____

What does this personal survey tell you about your thoughts and feelings about self-disclosure
with this person?

_____

_____

_____

Do you think your level of self-disclosure is appropriate or inappropriate with this person? Why?

_____

_____

_____

Harcourt Brace & Company

❖ 8.4 DEGREES OF SELF-DISCLOSURE ❖

◆ **Activity Type: Invitation to Insight**

PURPOSES

1. To demonstrate that self-disclosure can operate on a variety of levels, some quite intimate and others less revealing.
2. To give you practice in applying various types of self-disclosure to personal situations.

INSTRUCTIONS

For each of the following topics, write two statements for each level of self-disclosure. (See Chapter 8 of *Looking Out/Looking In* for descriptions of each level.)

EXAMPLE

Topic: School

1. Clichés
    a. *These exams sure are a drag!*
    b. *Textbooks sure are expensive!*

2. Facts
    a. *I'm a psychology major at the University of Oregon.*
    b. *I'm getting a teaching certificate so I'll be able to teach social studies.*

3. Opinions
    a. *I believe in affirmative action but I don't think there should be quotas for women and minorities.*
    b. *I don't think instructors should count class participation as part of a person's grade.*

4. Feelings
    a. *I feel scared when I think about the future. I'm almost finished with four years of college, and I'm still confused about what to do with my life.*
    b. *I get angry when Professor Autel doesn't prepare for our class.*

TOPIC: MY FAMILY

1. Clichés

    a. _____

    b. _____

2. Facts

    a. _____

    b. _____

3. Opinions

    a. _____

    b. _____

4. Feelings

    a. _____

    b. _____

TOPIC: MY CAREER PLANS

1. Clichés

    a. _____

    b. _____

2. Facts

    a._____

    b. _____

3. Opinions

    a. _____

    b. _____

4. Feelings

    a. _____

    b. _____

TOPIC: MY FRIENDSHIPS

1. Clichés

    a. _____

    b. _____

2. Facts

    a. _____

    b. _____

3. Opinions

   a. _____

   b. _____

4. Feelings

   a. _____

   b. _____

TOPIC: SPORTS

1. Clichés

   a. _____

   b. _____

2. Facts

   a. _____

   b. _____

3. Opinions

   a. _____

   b. _____

4. Feelings

   a. _____

   b. _____

Harcourt Brace & Company

✦ 8.5 RESPONSES IN RELATIONSHIPS ✦

❖ Activity Type: Skill Builder

PURPOSES

1. To generate responses to relational situations.
2. To evaluate the effectiveness and ethics of each situation.

INSTRUCTIONS

1. In groups, use the situations described below to record your possible words for each type of response listed.
2. Evaluate the effectiveness and ethics of your response.

EXAMPLE

Your friend asks you if you had a good time when you went out with his cousin last night.

Self-disclosure *I didn't have a great time, but then we were just getting to know one another. I don't think we had much in common.*

Partial disclosure *I had fun when we went to the movie.*

White lie or lie *Your cousin was a lot of fun and the movie was great.*

Hinting or equivocation *First dates are really times of discovery, aren't they?*

Which response is most effective/which most ethical? *I think the white lie was the most effective here. While I wasn't exactly truthful with my friend, I just don't want to tell him how boring I think his cousin is. I think it is better to just be nice to him and his cousin. Then both of them can save face, too.*

1. A family member calls and asks how you are doing in classes.

   Self-disclosure _____

   _____

   Partial disclosure _____

   _____

   White lie or lie _____

   _____

   Hinting or equivocation _____

   _____

   Which responses are most effective/which most ethical? ____

   _____

   _____

2. You are applying to rent an apartment that prohibits animals. You have a cat.

Self-disclosure _____

_____

Partial disclosure _____

_____

White lie or lie _____

_____

Hinting or equivocation _____

_____

Which responses are most effective/which most ethical? _____

_____

_____

3. You are being interviewed by a group of people to rent a room in the house they live in. They want to know if you are loud, clean, responsible, and the like.

Self-disclosure _____

_____

Partial disclosure _____

_____

White lie or lie _____

_____

Hinting or equivocation _____

_____

Which responses are most effective/which most ethical? _____

_____

_____

4. Your roommates ask what you think of the bright posters they've just put up around the room.

Self-disclosure _____

_____

Partial disclosure _____

_____

White lie or lie _____

_____

Hinting or equivocation _____

_____

Which responses are most effective/which most ethical? _____

_____

_____

5. Your romantic partner asks how many other people you've really loved before you met him or her.

Self-disclosure _____

_____

Partial disclosure _____

_____

White lie or lie _____

_____

Hinting or equivocation _____

_____

Which responses are most effective/which most ethical? _____

_____

_____

Harcourt Brace & Company

6. Your very opinionated father asks what you think of the people running for political office.

Self-disclosure _____

_____

Partial disclosure _____

_____

White lie or lie _____

_____

Hinting or equivocation _____

_____

Which responses are most effective/which most ethical? _____

_____

_____

7. Your boss at work wants to know what your plans for the future are.

Self-disclosure _____

_____

Partial disclosure _____

_____

White lie or lie _____

_____

Hinting or equivocation _____

_____

Which responses are most effective/which most ethical? _____

_____

_____

Harcourt Brace & Company

8. Your mother asks you about what your brother/sister has been up to lately.

Self-disclosure _____

_____

Partial disclosure _____

_____

White lie or lie _____

_____

Hinting or equivocation _____

_____

Which responses are most effective/which most ethical? _____

_____

_____

9. Your romantic partner wants to know why you are spending so much time with your other friends.

Self-disclosure _____

_____

Partial disclosure _____

_____

White lie or lie _____

_____

Hinting or equivocation _____

_____

Which responses are most effective/which most ethical? _____

_____

_____

Harcourt Brace & Company

❖ 8.6 RELATIONAL STAGES AND SELF-DISCLOSURE ❖

❖ Activity Type: Skill Builder

PURPOSES

1. To analyze different degrees of self-disclosure.
2. To discuss the appropriate levels of self-disclosure for different relational stages.

INSTRUCTIONS

1. In a group discuss the various situations listed below.
2. Identify the type of response that is likely (equivocation, lies, hinting, disclosure—include level such as fact or feeling).
3. Determine the function that response serves in the relationship.
4. Identify the relational stage(s) that may be illustrated by this type of response.

EXAMPLE

Two friends are discussing the effects of divorce in their families.

Type(s) of responses likely *Self-disclosure is likely to occur in this situation. Because they have similar experiences, the likelihood of reciprocity of self-disclosure is high. It will probably come from the highest levels of self-disclosure, feelings, but might also include a number of facts.*

Function in relationship *The self-disclosure functions to maintain the relationship, to increase intellectual and emotional intimacy, and to advance the stage of the relationship.*

Relational stage illustrated *This type of self-disclosure would most likely occur in an intensifying stage of a relationship, where the friends have gone beyond the small talk of experimenting and are beginning to develop more trust, more depth rather than breadth of self-disclosure, and where secrets are told and favors given.*

1. Friends are telling one another about their use of/refusal to use drugs.

   Type(s) of responses likely _____

   _____

   Function in relationship _____

   _____

   Relational stage illustrated _____

   _____

2. Two classmates are comparing their grades.

   Type(s) of responses likely _____

   _____

Function in relationship _____

_____

Relational stage illustrated _____

_____

3. A boyfriend and girlfriend are telling one another about their past romantic involvements.

Type(s) of responses likely _____

_____

Function in relationship _____

_____

Relational stage illustrated _____

_____

4. Two friends are shopping for clothes and giving one another advice on what looks good/bad.

Type(s) of responses likely _____

_____

Function in relationship _____

_____

Relational stage illustrated _____

_____

5. A parent asks a 20-year-old about his or her weekend.

Type(s) of responses likely _____

_____

Function in relationship _____

_____

Relational stage illustrated _____

_____

6. A manager and employee have agreed to sit down and talk about the problems they are experiencing with each other.

   Type(s) of responses likely _____

   _____

   Function in relationship _____

   _____

   Relational stage illustrated _____

   _____

7. A friend has just experienced a death in the family and the partner is expressing concern.

   Type(s) of responses likely _____

   _____

   Function in relationship _____

   _____

   Relational stage illustrated _____

   _____

8. Two acquaintances are exchanging their attitudes toward marriage.

   Type(s) of responses likely _____

   _____

   Function in relationship _____

   _____

   Relational stage illustrated _____

   _____

9. Two women are discussing childbearing.

   Type(s) of responses likely _____

   _____

Harcourt Brace & Company

Function in relationship _____

_____

Relational stage illustrated _____

_____

10. Two friends are discussing their worries and feelings of responsibility regarding their parents' advancing age.

Type(s) of responses likely_____

_____

Function in relationship _____

_____

Relational stage illustrated _____

_____

Harcourt Brace & Company

STUDY GUIDE

CHECK YOUR UNDERSTANDING

MATCHING (KEY TERM REVIEW)

Match the terms in column 1 with their definitions in column 2.

_____ 1. breadth

_____ 2. cliché

_____ 3. depth

_____ 4. dialectical tension

_____ 5. equivocal language

_____ 6. exchange theory

_____ 7. impression formation

_____ 8. intimacy

_____ 9. Johari Window

_____ 10. lie

_____ 11. manipulation

_____ 12. reciprocity

_____ 13. relational enhancement

_____ 14. self-disclosure

_____ 15. self-validation

_____ 16. small talk

_____ 17. social penetration

_____ 18. stages of relationships

_____ 19. uncertainty reduction

_____ 20. white lie

a. the state that exists when two opposing or incompatible forces exist simultaneously

b. a semieconomic model of relationships that suggests we often seek out people who can give us rewards that are greater than or equal to the costs we encounter in dealing with them

c. a model that describes relationships in terms of their breadth and depth

d. first dimension of self-disclosure involving the range of subjects being discussed

e. a model of relationships that describes broad phases of "coming together" and "coming apart"

f. speech that focuses on building beginning relationships, usually focusing on similarities with the other person

g. a deliberate attempt to hide or misrepresent the truth

h. a ritualized, stock statement delivered in response to a social situation

i. the process of getting to know others by gaining more information about them

j. a model that describes the relationship between self-disclosure and self-awareness

k. a dimension of self-disclosure involving a shift from relatively nonrevealing messages to more personal ones

l. a motivation for self-disclosing based on creating relational success by increasing honesty and depth of sharing

m. ambiguous language that has two or more equally plausible meanings

n. a deliberate hiding or misrepresentation of the truth, intended to help, or not to harm, the receiver

o. confirmation of a belief you hold about yourself

p. a motivation for self-disclosing based on the research evidence that individuals disclosing information about themselves encourage others to self-disclose in return

q. the process of deliberately revealing information about oneself that is significant and that would not normally be known by others

r. an act of self-disclosure calculated in advance to achieve a desired result

s. a state of personal sharing arising from physical, intellectual, or emotional contact

t. a relational process of revealing personal information to make ourselves more attractive

TRUE/FALSE

Mark the statements below as true or false. Correct statements that are false on the lines below to create a true statement.

_____   1. Intimacy is definitely rewarding, so maximizing intimacy is the best way of relating to others.

_____

_____

_____   2. The level of intimacy that feels right can change over time.

_____

_____

_____   3. Research shows that male-male relationships involve less disclosure than male-female or female-female relationships.

_____

_____

_____   4. Women are better at developing and maintaining intimate relationships than men.

_____

_____

_____   5. Germans and Japanese are more disclosing than members of any culture studied.

_____

_____

_____   6. There is a tendency for us to have a stronger dislike for offensive people whom we see as similar to us than for offensive people whom we see as different from us.

_____

_____

_____   7. People are most attracted to others who are competent, particularly those who appear not to have any flaws.

_____

_____

Harcourt Brace & Company

_____ 8. Intimacy is not the only goal of relationships.

_____

_____

_____ 9. Research indicates that partners in intimate relationships engage in high levels of self-disclosure frequently.

_____

_____

_____ 10. People justify over half of their lies as ways to avoid embarrassment for themselves or others.

_____

_____

COMPLETION

Fill in the blanks below with the correct terms chosen from the list below.

| open | hidden | blind | unknown | intellectual |
| physical | emotional | catharsis | hinting | attraction variable |

1. _____ is the type of intimacy that comes from an exchange of important ideas.

2. _____ is the type of intimacy that comes from touching, struggling, or sex.

3. _____ is the type of intimacy that comes from exchanging important feelings.

4. _____ is an explanation for what makes us want to develop personal relationships with some people and not with others.

5. _____ is a motivation for self-disclosing that allows you to "get it off your chest," to relieve yourself of uncomfortable secrecy.

6. _____ is a frame of the Johari Window that consists of information that you know about yourself but aren't willing to reveal to others.

7. _____ is a frame of the Johari Window that consists of information of which neither you nor the other person is aware.

8. _____ is a frame of the Johari Window that consists of information of which both you and the other person are aware.

Harcourt Brace & Company

9. _____ is a frame of the Johari Window that consists of information of which you are unaware but the other person in the relationship knows.

10. _____ is an alternative to self-disclosure in which the person gives only a clue to the direct meaning of the response.

MULTIPLE CHOICE

Place the letter of the developmental stage of the intimate relationship on the line before its example found below.

a. initiating
b. experimenting
c. intensifying
d. integrating
e. bonding

f. differentiating
g. circumscribing
h. stagnating
i. avoiding
j. terminating

_____ 1. A public ritual marks this stage.

_____ 2. First glances and "sizing up" each other typifies this stage.

_____ 3. Called the "we" stage, this stage involves increasing self-disclosure.

_____ 4. Lots of "small talk" typifies this stage.

_____ 5. This stage involves much focus on individual rather than dyadic interests.

_____ 6. There's very little growth or experimentation in this stage.

_____ 7. This stage involves much behavior that talks around the relational issues because the partners expect bad feelings.

_____ 8. The partners' social circles merge at this stage and they make purchases or commitments together.

_____ 9. No attempts are made to contact the other at this stage.

_____ 10. The relationship is redefined or dissolved at this stage.

_____ 11. A marriage ceremony would be typical here.

_____ 12. Roommates who make sure they are never in the same room and who are tolerating one another only until the lease is up might be at this stage.

_____ 13. A couple who avoids talking about future commitment because they are afraid of how the discussion will go is probably at this state.

_____ 14. This stage represents most communication at a social gathering where people are just getting to know one another.

_____ 15. In this stage, people spend an increasing amount of time together, asking for support from one another and doing favors for one another.

CHAPTER 8 STUDY GUIDE ANSWERS

MATCHING (KEY TERM REVIEW)

1. d	5. m	9. j	13. l	17. c
2. h	6. b	10. g	14. q	18. e
3. k	7. t	11. r	15. o	19. i
4. a	8. s	12. p	16. f	20. n

TRUE/FALSE

1. F	3. T	5. F	7. F	9. F
2. T	4. F	6. T	8. T	10. T

COMPLETION

1. intellectual	5. catharsis	9. blind
2. physical	6. hidden	10. hinting
3. emotional	7. unknown	
4. attraction variable	8. open	

MULTIPLE CHOICE

1. e	4. b	7. g	10. j	13. g
2. a	5. f	8. d	11. e	14. b
3. c	6. h	9. i	12. i	15. c

Harcourt Brace & Company

CHAPTER NINE

✛ Improving Communication Climates ✛

OUTLINE

Use this outline to take notes as you read the chapter in the text and/or as your instructor lectures in class.

I. **COMMUNICATION CLIMATE: THE KEY TO POSITIVE RELATIONSHIPS**
   A. **Confirming Communication**
      1. Recognition
      2. Acknowledgement
      3. Endorsement
   B. **Discomforting Communication**
      1. Verbal abuse
      2. Complaining
      3. Impervious response
      4. Interrupting response
      5. Irrelevant response
      6. Tangential response
      7. Impersonal response
      8. Ambiguous response
      9. Incongruous response
   C. **How Communication Climates Develop**
      1. Escalatory conflict spirals
      2. De-escalatory conflict spirals

II. **DEFENSIVENESS: CAUSES AND REMEDIES**
   A. **Causes: Face-Threatening Acts**
   B. **Types of Defensive Reactions**
      1. Attacking the critic
         a. Verbal aggression
         b. Sarcasm
      2. Distorting critical information
         a. Rationalization
         b. Compensation
         c. Regression

3. Avoiding dissonant information
   a. Physical avoidance
   b. Repression
   c. Apathy
   d. Displacement
C. **Preventing Defensiveness in Others**
   1. Evaluation versus description
   2. Control versus problem orientation
   3. Strategy versus spontaneity
   4. Neutrality versus empathy
   5. Superiority versus equality
   6. Certainty versus provisionalism
D. **Responding Nondefensively to Criticism**
   1. Seek more information
      a. Ask for specifics
      b. Guess about specifics
      c. Paraphrase the speaker's ideas
      d. Ask what the critic wants
      e. Ask about the consequences of your behavior
      f. Ask what else is wrong
   2. Agree with the critic
      a. Agree with the truth
      b. Agree with the critic's perception

KEY TERMS

Use these key terms to review major concepts from your text. Write the definition for each key term in the space to the right.

acknowledgment _____

ambiguous response _____

apathy _____

certainty _____

cognitive dissonance _____

communication climate _____

compensation _____

complaining _____

confirming communication _____

controlling communication _____

Harcourt Brace & Company

criticism _____

de-escalatory conflict spirals _____

defense mechanism _____

defensiveness _____

descriptive communication _____

disconfirming communication _____

displacement _____

empathy _____

endorsement _____

equality _____

escalatory conflict spirals _____

evaluative communication _____

face-threatening act _____

Gibb categories _____

impersonal response _____

impervious response _____

incongruous response _____

indifference _____

interrupting response _____

irrelevant response _____

neutrality _____

physical avoidance _____

problem orientation _____

provisionalism _____

rationalization _____

Harcourt Brace & Company

recognition _____

regression _____

repression _____

sarcasm _____

spiral _____

spontaneity _____

strategy _____

superiority _____

tangential response _____

verbal abuse _____

verbal aggression _____

ACTIVITIES

❖ 9.1 UNDERSTANDING YOUR DEFENSIVE RESPONSES ❖

◆ Activity Type: Invitation to Insight

PURPOSE

To help you identify your typical defensive responses.

INSTRUCTIONS

1. Identify the person or people who would be most likely to deliver each of the following critical messages to you. If you are unlikely to hear one or more of the following messages, substitute a defensiveness-arousing topic of your own.
2. For each situation, describe
   a. the person likely to deliver the message.
   b. the typical content of the message.
   c. the general type of response(s) you make: attacking, distorting, or avoiding.
   d. your typical verbal response(s).
   e. your typical nonverbal response(s).
   f. the part of your presenting self being defended.
   g. the probable consequences of these response(s).

EXAMPLE

A negative comment about your use of time.
Person likely to deliver this message *my parents* _____
Typical content of the message *wasting my time watching TV instead of studying* _____
General type(s) of response *attacking, distorting* _____
Your typical verbal response(s) *"Get off my back! I work hard! I need time to relax." "I'll study later;*
I've got plenty of time." _____
Your typical nonverbal response(s) *harsh tone of voice, sullen silence for an hour or two*
Part of presenting self being defended *good student, not lazy* _____
Probable consequences of your response(s) *uncomfortable silence, more criticism from parents in*
the future _____

1. Negative comment about your appearance.

   Person likely to deliver this message _____

   Typical content of the message _____

   _____

   General type(s) of response _____

Your typical verbal response(s) _____

_____

Your typical nonverbal response(s) _____

_____

Part(s) of presenting self being defended _____

Probable consequences of your response(s) _____

_____

_____

2. Criticism about your choice of friends.

Person likely to deliver this message _____

Typical content of the message _____

_____

General type(s) of response _____

Your typical verbal response(s) _____

_____

Your typical nonverbal response(s) _____

_____

Part(s) of presenting self being defended _____

Probable consequences of your response(s) _____

_____

_____

3. Criticism of a job you've just completed.

Person likely to deliver this message _____

Typical content of the message _____

_____

Harcourt Brace & Company

General type(s) of response _____

Your typical verbal response(s) _____

_____

Your typical nonverbal response(s) _____

_____

Part(s) of presenting self being defended _____

Probable consequences of your response(s) _____

_____

_____

4. Criticism of your schoolwork.

Person likely to deliver this message _____

Typical content of the message _____

_____

General type(s) of response _____

Your typical verbal response(s) _____

_____

Your typical nonverbal response(s) _____

_____

Part(s) of presenting self being defended _____

Probable consequences of your response(s) _____

_____

_____

5. Criticism of your diet or eating habits.

Person likely to deliver this message _____

Typical content of the message _____

_____

General type(s) of response _____

Your typical verbal response(s) _____

_____

Your typical nonverbal response(s) _____

_____

Part(s) of presenting self being defended _____

Probable consequences of your response(s) _____

_____

_____

6. A negative comment about your exercise (or lack of it).

Person likely to deliver this message _____

Typical content of the message _____

_____

General type(s) of response _____

Your typical verbal response(s) _____

_____

Your typical nonverbal response(s) _____

_____

Part(s) of presenting self being defended _____

Probable consequences of your response(s) _____

_____

_____

Harcourt Brace & Company

❖ 9.2 DEFENSIVE AND SUPPORTIVE LANGUAGE ❖

◆❖ Activity Type: Skill Builder

PURPOSE

To help you recognize the difference between the Gibb categories of defensive and supportive language.

INSTRUCTIONS

1. For each of the situations below, write two statements a speaker might make. One should contain evaluative language and the other descriptive language.
2. In the space adjacent to each statement, label the Gibb categories of language that your words represent.

EXAMPLE

A neighbor's late-night stereo music playing is disrupting your sleep.

Defense-arousing statement *Why don't you show a little consideration and turn that damn thing down? If I hear any more noise I'm going to call the police!*

Type(s) of defensive language *evaluation, control*

Supportive statement *When I hear your stereo music late at night I can't sleep, which leaves me more and more tired. I'd like to figure out some way you can listen and I can sleep.*

Type(s) of supportive language *description, problem orientation*

1. It is two o'clock in the morning, and the parents of a teenager have been waiting up for the arrival of their son or daughter, who was expected home by midnight.

   Defense-arousing statement _____

   _____

   _____

   _____

   Type(s) of defensive language _____

   Supportive statement _____

   _____

   _____

   _____

   Type(s) of supportive language _____

Harcourt Brace & Company

2. You and your roommate split the cost of groceries and share food. Recently, however, your roommate has been bringing guests over and feasting on your food supply.

Defense-arousing statement _____

_____

_____

_____

Type(s) of defensive language _____

Supportive statement _____

_____

_____

_____

Type(s) of supportive language _____

3. A boss criticizes an employee for being late to work. The employee explains that he or she has been having car trouble.

Defense-arousing statement _____

_____

_____

_____

Type(s) of defensive language _____

Supportive statement _____

_____

_____

_____

Type(s) of supportive language _____

Harcourt Brace & Company

4. A teacher is explaining the Gibb categories to a student who is having difficulty understanding them.

Defense-arousing statement _____

_____

_____

_____

Type(s) of defensive language _____

Supportive statement _____

_____

_____

_____

Type(s) of supportive language _____

5. Two people are debating whether or not capital punishment is an appropriate means of preventing serious crimes.

Defense-arousing statement _____

_____

_____

_____

Type(s) of defensive language _____

Supportive statement _____

_____

_____

_____

Type(s) of supportive language _____

Harcourt Brace & Company

6. On many occasions a friend drops by your place without calling first. Since you often have other plans, this behavior puts you in an uncomfortable position.

Defense-arousing statement _____

_____

_____

_____

Type(s) of defensive language _____

Supportive statement _____

_____

_____

_____

Type(s) of supportive language _____

7. (Record a situation of your own here.) _____

_____

Defense-arousing statement _____

_____

_____

_____

Type(s) of defensive language _____

Supportive statement _____

_____

_____

_____

Type(s) of supportive language _____

❖ 9.3 COPING WITH TYPICAL CRITICISM ❖

❖ Activity Type: Skill Builder

PURPOSE

To help you practice nondefensive responses to typical criticisms you may face.

INSTRUCTIONS

1. For each situation below, write a nondefensive response you could use that follows the guidelines of seeking more information or agreeing with the critic described in Chapter 9 of *Looking Out/Looking In.*
2. Join with two partners and identify the members as A, B, and C.
3. Role-play situations 1 and 2 with A responding to the criticisms offered by B, while C uses *9.4 Coping with Criticism* to evaluate A's behavior.
4. Switch roles so that B responds to C's criticisms on items 3 and 4, while A completes the checklist.
5. Switch roles again so that C responds to A's criticisms on items 5 and 6, while B completes the checklist.

Situation	How I Could Respond Effectively to This Criticism
1. You've been late to work every day this week. Just who do you think you are that you can come wandering in after the rest of us are already working?	
2. This place is a mess! Don't you care about how we live?	
3. No wonder your grades are low. You're always out partying instead of studying.	
4. Your sister got terrific grades this term.	

Situation	How I Could Respond Effectively to This Criticism
5. How could you have been so thoughtless at the party last night?	
6. It takes you so long to get the idea.	
7. You think I'm your personal servant!	
8. Haven't you finished that yet?	
9. What's the matter with you? You've been so cold lately.	
10. Why can't your children be quiet like theirs?	
11. You should have consulted somebody before acting on that.	
12. Your motivation level sure is low lately.	

✤ 9.4 COPING WITH CRITICISM ✤

❖ Activity Type: Oral Skill

PURPOSE

To practice nondefensive responses to criticisms.

INSTRUCTIONS

1. Form triads and identify members as A, B, and C.
2. Person A describes a common defensiveness-arousing criticism he or she faces, identifying the critic, topic, and the critic's behavior.
3. Person B paraphrases and questions A until he or she understands the critic's behavior.
4. Persons A and B then role-play the situation, with A practicing the skills of seeking more information and agreeing with the critic as described in Chapter 9 of *Looking Out/Looking In*.
5. Person C uses *Coping with Criticism* to evaluate A's skill at responding nondefensively.
6. After the role-play, person C provides feedback to person A.
7. Rotate roles and repeat steps 1–6 until both B and C have had the chance to practice responding nondefensively to criticism.

CHECKLIST

5 = superior   4 = excellent   3 = good   2 = fair   1 = poor

Seeks additional information to understand criticism and critic

—asks for specific details of criticism   _____

—guesses about specific details when critic does not supply facts   _____

—paraphrases critic to clarify criticism and draw out more information   _____

—asks what the critic wants   _____

—asks critic to describe the consequences of behavior
("How does my behavior [be specific] cause problems for you?")   _____

—asks what else is wrong   _____

Agrees as appropriate with criticism

—agrees with facts (truth only)

—agrees with critic's right to perceive event differently
("I can understand why it looks that way to you because . . .")   _____

Maintains appropriate nonverbal behaviors to indicate sincerity   _____
—voice
—facial expression
—posture and gestures
—body orientation and distance

Total   _____

Harcourt Brace & Company

STUDY GUIDE

CHECK YOUR UNDERSTANDING

MATCHING (KEY TERM REVIEW)

Match the terms in column 1 with their definitions in column 2.

_____ 1. ambiguous response	a. a defense mechanism in which a person avoids admitting emotional pain by pretending not to care about an event
_____ 2. apathy	
_____ 3. cognitive dissonance	b. a reciprocating communication pattern in which the parties slowly lessen their dependence on one another, withdraw, and become less invested in the relationship
_____ 4. communication climate	
_____ 5. compensation	c. a defense mechanism in which a person stresses a strength in one area to camouflage a shortcoming in some other area
_____ 6. complaining	
_____ 7. confirming communication	d. an inconsistency between two conflicting pieces of information, attitudes, or behavior
_____ 8. controlling communication	
_____ 9. de-escalatory conflict spiral	e. a psychological device used to maintain a presenting self-image that an individual believes is threatened
_____ 10. defense mechanism	f. a message that expresses a lack of caring or respect for another person
_____ 11. disconfirming communication	g. a reciprocal communication pattern in which one attack leads to another until the initial skirmish grows into a full-fledged battle
_____ 12. displacement	
_____ 13. escalatory conflict spiral	h. a disconfirming response with more than one meaning, leaving the other party unsure of the responder's position
_____ 14. face-threatening act	i. behavior by another that is perceived as attacking an individual's presenting image, or face
_____ 15. impersonal response	
_____ 16. impervious response	j. a disconfirming response that is superficial or trite
_____ 17. incongruous response	k. a disconfirming response that ignores another person's attempt to communicate

Harcourt Brace & Company

_____ 18. interrupting response

_____ 19. irrelevant response

_____ 20. rationalization

l. the emotional tone of a relationship between two or more individuals

m. a disconfirming response in which one communicator's comments bear no relationship to the previous speaker's ideas

n. a disconfirming response that implicitly or explicitly attributes responsibility for the speaker's displeasure to another party

o. a defense mechanism in which logical but untrue explanations maintain an unrealistic desired or presenting self-image

p. a disconfirming response in which two messages, one of which is usually nonverbal, contradict one another

q. a message that expresses caring or respect for another person

r. a disconfirming response in which one communicator breaks into the other's communication

s. messages in which the sender tries to impose some sort of outcome on the receiver, usually resulting in a defensive reaction

t. a defense mechanism in which a person vents hostile or aggressive feelings on a target that cannot strike back, instead of on the true target

TRUE/FALSE

Mark the statements below as true or false. Correct statements that are false on the lines below to create a true statement.

_____ 1. The tone or climate of a relationship is shaped by the degree to which the people believe themselves to be valued by one another.

_____

_____

_____ 2. Disagreeing with another person is always disconfirming or defense-arousing.

_____

_____

_____ 3. Most experts agree that it is psychologically healthier to have someone ignore you than disagree with you.

_____

_____

Harcourt Brace & Company

_____ 4. Both positive and negative communication spirals have their limits; they rarely go on indefinitely.

_____

_____

_____ 5. When the criticism leveled at us is accurate, we will not get defensive.

_____

_____

_____ 6. Communicators strive to resolve inconsistencies or conflicting pieces of information because this "dissonant" condition is uncomfortable.

_____

_____

_____ 7. Using Jack Gibb's supportive behaviors will eliminate defensiveness in your receivers.

_____

_____

_____ 8. According to your text, spontaneity can sometimes be used as a strategy.

_____

_____

_____ 9. When you truly understand hostile comments, you just naturally accept them.

_____

_____

_____ 10. In order to cope with criticism, you should agree with all the critics' statements.

_____

_____

Harcourt Brace & Company

COMPLETION

The Gibb categories of defensive and supportive behavior are six sets of contrasting styles of verbal and nonverbal behavior. Each set describes a communication style that is likely to arouse defensiveness and a contrasting style that is likely to prevent or reduce it. Fill in the blanks with the Gibb behavior described chosen from the list below.

evaluation	description	control	problem orientation	strategy
spontaneity	neutrality	empathy	superiority	equality
certainty	provisionalism			

1. _____ is the attitude behind messages that dogmatically imply that the speaker's position is correct and that the other person's ideas are not worth considering.

2. _____ is communication behavior involving messages that describe the speaker's position without evaluating others.

3. _____ is a supportive style of communication in which the communicators focus on working together to solve their problems instead of trying to impose their own solutions on one another.

4. _____ is a defense-arousing style of communication in which the sender tries to manipulate or deceive a receiver.

5. _____ is a supportive style of communication in which the sender expresses a willingness to consider the other person's position.

6. _____ is a defense-arousing style of communication in which the sender states or implies that the receiver is not worthy of respect.

7. _____ is a supportive communication behavior in which the sender expresses a message openly and honestly without any attempt to manipulate the receiver.

8. _____ is a defense-arousing behavior in which the sender expresses indifference toward a receiver.

9. _____ is a defense-arousing message in which the sender tries to impose some sort of outcome on the receiver.

10. _____ is a type of supportive communication that suggests that the sender regards the receiver as worthy of respect.

Harcourt Brace & Company

MULTIPLE CHOICE

Choose the letter of the defensive or supportive category that is best illustrated by each of the situations below.

a. evaluation	g. description
b. control	h. problem orientation
c. strategy	i. spontaneity
d. neutrality	j. empathy
e. superiority	k. equality
f. certainty	l. provisionalism

_____ 1. Gerry insists he has all the facts and needs to hear no more information.

_____ 2. Richard has a strong opinion but will listen to another position.

_____ 3. Lina kept looking at the clock as she was listening to Nan, so Nan thought Lina didn't consider her comments as very important.

_____ 4. "I know Janice doesn't agree with me," Mary said, "but she knows how strongly I feel about this, and I think she understands my position."

_____ 5. "Even though my professor has a Ph.D.," Rosa pointed out, "she doesn't act like she's the only one who knows something; she is really interested in me as a person."

_____ 6. "When I found out that Bob had tricked me into thinking his proposal was my idea so I'd support it, I was really angry."

_____ 7. "Even though we *all* wait tables here, Evanne thinks she's better than any of us— just look at the way she prances around!"

_____ 8. Clara sincerely and honestly told Georgia about her reservations concerning Georgia's planned party.

_____ 9. The co-workers attempted to find a solution to the scheduling issue that would satisfy both of their needs.

_____ 10. "It seems as though my father's favorite phrase is `I know what's best for you' and that really gripes me."

_____ 11. "You drink too much."

_____ 12. "I was embarrassed when you slurred your speech in front of my boss."

_____ 13. "The flowers and presents are just an attempt to get me to go to bed with him."

_____ 14. "She looked down her nose at me when I told her I didn't exercise regularly."

_____ 15. "Well, if you need more money and I need more help around here, what could we do to make us both happy?"

Harcourt Brace & Company

Choose the letter of the type of coping with criticism that is best illustrated by each of the situations below.

    a. ask for specific details of criticism
    b. guess about specific details
    c. paraphrase to clarify criticism
    d. ask what the critic wants
    e. ask critic to describe the consequences of behavior
    f. ask what else is wrong
    g. agree with true facts
    h. agree with critic's right to perceive differently

Criticism: "You never seem to care about much."

_____ 16. "Are you referring to my not going to the office party?"

_____ 17. "You're right that I didn't call you back within 24 hours."

_____ 18. "What do you want me to care more about?"

_____ 19. "I can see why you'd be upset with me for not coming to the party because you've told me you want me to be more involved with your work's social events."

_____ 20. "When I didn't come to the party, were you embarrassed or something?"

_____ 21. "So not calling you back right away was a problem. Have I upset you any other way?"

_____ 22. "So you're upset that I'm not visiting you every week, and you think that shows a lack of affection on my part—is that it?"

_____ 23. "So if I don't return your call right away, what happens?"

_____ 24. "You're correct in that I couldn't visit this week because of finals."

_____ 25. "Because I wasn't at the party, it reflected badly on you?"

CHAPTER 9 STUDY GUIDE ANSWERS

MATCHING (KEY TERM REVIEW)

1.	h	5.	c	9.	b	13.	g	17.	p
2.	a	6.	n	10.	e	14.	i	18.	r
3.	d	7.	q	11.	f	15.	j	19.	m
4.	l	8.	s	12.	t	16.	k	20.	o

TRUE/FALSE

1.	T	3.	F	5.	F	7.	F	9.	F
2.	F	4.	T	6.	T	8.	T	10.	F

COMPLETION

1. certainty
2. description
3. problem orientation
4. strategy
5. provisionalism
6. superiority
7. spontaneity
8. neutrality
9. control
10. equality

MULTIPLE CHOICE

1.	f	6.	c	11.	a	16.	a	21.	f
2.	l	7.	e	12.	g	17.	g	22.	c
3.	d	8.	i	13.	c	18.	d	23.	e
4.	j	9.	h	14.	e	19.	h	24.	g
5.	k	10.	b	15.	h	20.	b	25.	b

Harcourt Brace & Company

❖ Managing Interpersonal Conflicts ❖

OUTLINE

Use this outline to take notes as you read the chapter in the text and/or as your instructor lectures in class.

I. **THE NATURE OF CONFLICT**
   A. **Definition**
      1. Expressed struggle
      2. Perceived incompatible goals
      3. Perceived scarce rewards
   B. **Conflict Is Natural**
   C. **Conflict Can Be Beneficial**

II. **PERSONAL CONFLICT STYLES**
   A. **Nonassertion**
      1. Avoidance
      2. Accommodation
   B. **Direct Aggression**
   C. **Passive Aggression—Crazymaking**
   D. **Indirect Communication**
   E. **Assertion**
   F. **Determining the Best Style**
      1. Situation
      2. Receiver
      3. Your goals

III. **ASSERTION WITHOUT AGGRESSION: THE CLEAR MESSAGE FORMAT**
   A. **Behavior**
   B. **Interpretation**
   C. **Feeling**
   D. **Consequence**
      1. What happens to you, the speaker
      2. What happens to the person you're addressing
      3. What happens to others

Harcourt Brace & Company

E. **Intention**
1. Where you stand on an issue
2. Requests of others
3. Descriptions of how you plan to act in the future

F. **Using the Clear Message Format**
1. May be delivered in mixed order
2. Word to suit your personal style
3. Combine elements when appropriate
4. Take your time delivering the message

IV. **CONFLICT IN RELATIONAL SYSTEMS**
A. **Complementary, Symmetrical, and Parallel Styles**
B. **Intimate and Aggressive Styles**
C. **Conflict Rituals**

V. **VARIABLES IN CONFLICT STYLES**
A. **Gender**
B. **Culture**

VI. **STYLES OF CONFLICT RESOLUTION**
A. **Win–Lose**
B. **Lose–Lose**
C. **Compromise**
D. **Win–Win**

VII. **WIN–WIN COMMUNICATION SKILLS**
A. **Identify Your Problem and Unmet Needs**
B. **Make a Date**
C. **Describe Your Problem and Needs**
D. **Consider Your Partner's Point of View**
E. **Negotiate a Solution**
1. Identify and define the conflict
2. Generate a number of possible solutions
3. Evaluate the alternative solutions
4. Decide on the best solution
F. **Follow Up on the Solution**

VIII. **CONSTRUCTIVE CONFLICT: QUESTIONS AND ANSWERS**
A. **Isn't Win–Win Too Good to Be True?**
B. **Isn't Win–Win Too Elaborate?**
C. **Isn't Win–Win Negotiating *Too* Rational?**
D. **Is It Possible to Change Others?**

Harcourt Brace & Company

KEY TERMS

Use these key terms to review major concepts from your text. Write the definition for each key term in the space to the right.

accommodation _____

aggressive conflict style _____

assertion _____

avoidance _____

behavioral description _____

clear message format _____

complementary conflict style _____

compromise _____

conflict _____

conflict ritual _____

consequence statement _____

crazymaking _____

direct aggression _____

feeling statement _____

indirect communication _____

intention statement _____

interdependence _____

interpretation _____

intimate conflict style _____

lose–lose problem solving _____

negotiation _____

no-lose problem solving _____

Harcourt Brace & Company

nonassertion _____

parallel conflict style _____

passive aggression _____

relational conflict style _____

scarce rewards _____

struggle _____

symmetrical conflict style _____

win–lose problem solving _____

win–win problem solving _____

ACTIVITIES

❖ 10.1 UNDERSTANDING CONFLICT STYLES ❖
◆❖ Activity Type: Skill Builder

PURPOSE

To help you understand the styles with which conflicts can be handled.

INSTRUCTIONS

1. For each of the conflicts described below, write four responses illustrating nonassertive, directly aggressive, passive aggressive, indirect communication, and assertive communication styles.
2. Describe the probable consequences of each style.

EXAMPLE

Three weeks ago your friend borrowed an article of clothing, promising to return it soon. You haven't seen it since, and the friend hasn't mentioned it.

Nonassertive response *Say nothing to the friend, hoping she will remember and return the item.*

Probable consequences *There's a good chance I'll never get the item back. I would probably resent the friend and avoid her in the future so I won't have to lend anything else.*

Directly aggressive response *Confront the friend and accuse her of being inconsiderate and irresponsible. Say that she probably ruined the item and is afraid to say so.*

Probable consequences *My friend would get defensive and hurt. Even if she did intentionally keep the item, she'd never admit it when approached this way. We would probably avoid each other in the future.*

Passive aggressive response *Complain to another friend, knowing it will get back to her.*

Probable consequences *My friend might be embarrassed by my gossip and be even more resistant to return it.*

Indirect communication *Drop hints about how I loved to wear the borrowed item. Casually mention how much I hate people who don't return things.*

Probable consequences *My friend might ignore my hints. She'll most certainly resent my roundabout approach, even if she returns the article.*

Assertive response *Confront the friend in a noncritical way and remind her that she still has the item. Ask when she'll return it, being sure to get a specific time.*

Probable consequences *The friend might be embarrassed when I bring the subject up, but since there's no attack it'll probably be okay. Since we'll have cleared up the problem, the relationship can continue.*

1. Someone you've just met at a party criticizes a mutual friend in a way you think is unfair.

   Nonassertive response _____

   _____

   _____

   Probable consequences _____

   _____

   Directly aggressive response _____

   _____

   _____

   Probable consequences _____

   _____

   Passive aggressive response _____

   _____

   _____

   Probable consequences _____

   _____

   Indirect communication _____

   _____

   _____

   Probable consequences _____

   _____

   Assertive response _____

   _____

   _____

   Probable consequences _____

   _____

Harcourt Brace & Company

2. A fan behind you at a ballgame toots a loud air horn every time the home team makes any progress. The noise is spoiling your enjoyment of the game.

Nonassertive response _____

_____

_____

Probable consequences _____

_____

Directly aggressive response _____

_____

_____

Probable consequences _____

_____

Passive aggressive response _____

_____

_____

Probable consequences _____

_____

Indirect communication _____

_____

_____

Probable consequences _____

_____

Assertive response _____

_____

_____

Probable consequences _____

_____

3. Earlier in the day you asked the person with whom you live to stop by the store and pick up snacks for a party you are having this evening. Your roommate arrives home without the food, and it's too late to return to the store.

Nonassertive response _____

_____

_____

Probable consequences _____

_____

Directly aggressive response _____

_____

_____

Probable consequences _____

_____

Passive aggressive response _____

_____

_____

Probable consequences _____

_____

Indirect communication _____

_____

_____

Probable consequences _____

_____

Assertive response _____

_____

_____

Probable consequences _____

_____

Harcourt Brace & Company

4. You are explaining your political views to a friend who has asked your opinion. Now the friend obviously isn't listening. You think to yourself that since the person asked for your ideas, the least he or she can do is pay attention.

Nonassertive response _____

_____

_____

Probable consequences _____

_____

Directly aggressive response _____

_____

_____

Probable consequences _____

_____

Passive aggressive response _____

_____

_____

Probable consequences _____

_____

Indirect communication _____

_____

_____

Probable consequences _____

_____

Assertive response _____

_____

_____

Probable consequences _____

_____

Harcourt Brace & Company

5. You find out that a friend at work told other people with whom you work some very personal information about you.

Nonassertive response _____

_____

_____

Probable consequences _____

_____

Directly aggressive response _____

_____

_____

Probable consequences _____

_____

Passive aggressive response _____

_____

_____

Probable consequences _____

_____

Indirect communication _____

_____

_____

Probable consequences _____

_____

Assertive response _____

_____

_____

Probable consequences _____

_____

Harcourt Brace & Company

❖ 10.2 WRITING CLEAR MESSAGES ❖

◆❖ Activity Type: Skill Builder

PURPOSE

To help you turn unclear messages into clear ones.

INSTRUCTIONS

Imagine a situation in which you might have said each of the statements below. Rewrite the messages in the clear message format, being sure to include each of the five elements described in your text.

EXAMPLE

Unclear message: "It's awful when you can't trust a friend."

Clear message:

Lena, when I gave you the keys to my house so you could borrow those clothes _____ (behavior)

I figured .you'd know to lock up again when you left. _____ (interpretation)

I was worried and scared _____ (feeling)

because I found the door unlocked and thought there was a break-in. _____ (consequence)

I want to know if you left the house open and, let you know how upset I am. _____ (intention)

1. "Blast it, Robin! Get off my back."

   _____ (behavior)

   _____ (interpretation)

   _____ (feeling)

   _____ (consequence)

   _____ (intention)

2. "I wish you'd pay more attention to me."

   _____ (behavior)

   _____ (interpretation)

   _____ (feeling)

   _____ (consequence)

   _____ (intention)

3. "You've sure been thoughtful lately."

_____ (behavior)

_____ (interpretation)

_____ (feeling)

_____ (consequence)

_____ (intention)

4. "Nobody's perfect!"

_____ (behavior)

_____ (interpretation)

_____ (feeling)

_____ (consequence)

_____ (intention)

5. "Matt, you're such a slob!"

_____ (behavior)

_____ (interpretation)

_____ (feeling)

_____ (consequence)

_____ (intention)

6. "Let's just forget it; with all the screaming, I get flustered."

_____ (behavior)

_____ (interpretation)

_____ (feeling)

_____ (consequence)

_____ (intention)

Harcourt Brace & Company

7. "I really shouldn't eat any of that cake you baked."

_____ (behavior)

_____ (interpretation)

_____ (feeling)

_____ (consequence)

_____ (intention)

Now list three significant messages that you could send to important people in your life: complaints, requests, or expressions of appreciation. Write them in clear message format.

8. _____ (behavior)

_____ (interpretation)

_____ (feeling)

_____ (consequence)

_____ (intention)

9. _____ (behavior)

_____ (interpretation)

_____ (feeling)

_____ (consequence)

_____ (intention)

10. _____ (behavior)

_____ (interpretation)

_____ (feeling)

_____ (consequence)

_____ (intention)

Harcourt Brace & Company

✛ 10.3 YOUR CONFLICT STYLES ✛

◆ Activity Type: Invitation to Insight

PURPOSE

To help you identify the styles you use to handle conflicts.

INSTRUCTIONS

1. Use the form below to record the conflicts that occur in your life. Describe any minor issues which arise as well as major problems.
2. For each incident, describe your conflict style, your approach to resolution, and the consequences of these behaviors.
3. Summarize your findings in the space provided.

Harcourt Brace & Company

Incident	Your Behavior	Your Conflict Style	Approach to Resolution	Consequences
Example My friend accused me of being too negative about the possibility of finding rewarding, well-paying work.	I became defensive and angrily denied his claim. In turn I accused him of being too critical.	Direct aggression	Win–lose	After arguing for some time, we left each other, both feeling upset. I'm sure we'll both feel awkward around each other for a while.
1.				
2.				

Incident	Your Behavior	Your Conflict Style	Approach to Resolution	Consequences
3.				
4.				
5.				

Harcourt Brace & Company

CONCLUSIONS

Are there any individuals or issues that repeatedly arouse conflicts?

_____

_____

What conflict style(s) do you most commonly use? Do you use different styles with different people or in different situations? Describe.

_____

_____

_____

_____

_____

_____

What approaches do you usually take in resolving conflicts? Do you use different approaches depending on the people or situations? Describe.

_____

_____

_____

What are the consequences of the behaviors you described above? Are you satisfied with them? If not, how could you change?

_____

_____

_____

_____

Harcourt Brace & Company

❖ 10.4 WIN–WIN PROBLEM SOLVING ❖

◆❖ Activity Type: Invitation to Insight

PURPOSE

To help you apply the win–win problem-solving method to a personal conflict.

INSTRUCTIONS

1. Follow the instructions below as a guide to dealing with an interpersonal conflict facing you now.
2. After completing the no-lose steps, record your conclusions in the space provided.

Step 1: Identify your unmet needs.

_____

_____

_____

_____

Step 2: Make a date. (Choose a time and place that will make it easiest for both parties to work constructively on the issue.)

_____

_____

_____

_____

Step 3: Describe your problem and needs. (Use behavior—interpret—feel—consequence—intend format, but avoid proposing specific means or solutions at this point.)

_____

_____

_____

_____

Harcourt Brace & Company

Step 4: Consider your partner's point of view. (Ask your partner what he or she wants and check your understanding—paraphrase or perception—check as necessary.)

_____

_____

_____

_____

Step 5: Negotiate a solution.

a. Restate the needs of both parties, just to be sure they are clear.

_____

_____

_____

_____

b. Work together to generate a number of possible solutions that might satisfy these needs. Don't criticize any suggestions here!

_____

_____

_____

_____

_____

_____

c. Evaluate the solutions you just listed, considering the advantages and problems of each. If you think of any new solutions, record them above.

_____

_____

_____

_____

Harcourt Brace & Company

d.   Decide on the best solution, listing it here.

_____

_____

_____

Step 6: Follow up the solution. After a trial period, meet with your partner and see if your agreement is satisfying both your needs. If not, return to step 3 and use this procedure to refine your solution.

_____

_____

_____

_____

CONCLUSIONS

In what ways did this procedure differ from the way in which you usually deal with interpersonal conflicts?

_____

_____

_____

_____

Was the outcome of your problem-solving session different from what it might have been if you had communicated in your usual style? How?

_____

_____

_____

_____

In what ways can you use the no-lose methods in your interpersonal conflicts? With whom? On what issues? What kinds of behavior will be especially important?

_____

_____

_____

_____

Harcourt Brace & Company

❖ 10.5 CONFLICT RESOLUTION DYADS ❖

❖ **Activity Type: Oral Skill**

PURPOSE

To develop your skills in using the assertive, win–win conflict resolution methods introduced in Chapter 10 of *Looking Out/Looking In.*

INSTRUCTIONS

1. Join with three partners and identify the members as A, B, C, and D.
2. A and B choose a conflict from their own lives or from the list below and role-play conflict, using the assertive, win–win conflict resolution methods introduced in Chapter 10 of *Looking Out/Looking In.*
3. During the role-playing situation, C uses the *Checklist* below to evaluate A's communication skill, while D uses the checklist to evaluate B's skill.
4. After the role-play, C provides feedback to A, and D provides feedback to B.
5. Switch roles so that C and D role-play a conflict, while A and B complete the checklist and provide feedback to C and D.

ISSUES

household chores   academic grades   budgeting

use of language offensive to one partner; use of alcohol, drugs, etc.
exclusive versus nonexclusive dating or friendships
how much time to spend with/apart from each other
parental involvement in offspring's life
use of equipment or clothing belonging to one partner

CHECKLIST   5 = superior   4 = excellent   3 = good   2 = fair   1 = poor

Makes a date   _____

Describes problem and needs   _____
   —behavior
   —interpretations
   —feelings
   —consequences
   —intentions

Considers partner's point of view/solicits partner's understanding   _____

Paraphrases/perception checks to verify understanding of partner's needs   _____

Negotiates win–win solution to best possible extent   _____
   —identifies/summarizes conflict
   —generates possible solutions without premature evaluation
   —evaluates alternatives
   —decides on win–win solution

Plans follow-up meeting to modify solution as necessary.   _____

                                                                       TOTAL   _____

STUDY GUIDE

CHECK YOUR UNDERSTANDING

MATCHING (KEY TERM REVIEW)

Match the terms in column 1 with their definitions in column 2.

_____ 1. accommodation

_____ 2. assertion

_____ 3. avoidance

_____ 4. complementary conflict style

_____ 5. compromise

_____ 6. conflict

_____ 7. conflict ritual

_____ 8. consequence statement

_____ 9. direct aggression

_____ 10. indirect communication

_____ 11. intention statement

_____ 12. lose–lose problem solving

_____ 13. negotiation

_____ 14. nonassertion

_____ 15. parallel conflict style

_____ 16. passive aggression

_____ 17. relational conflict style

_____ 18. symmetrical conflict style

a. a direct expression of the sender's needs, thoughts, or feelings, delivered in a way that does not attack the receiver's dignity

b. a criticism or demand that threatens the face of the person to whom it is directed

c. an approach to conflict resolution in which both parties attain at least part of what they wanted through self-sacrifice

d. a nonassertive response style in which the communicator is unwilling to confront a situation in which his or her needs are not being met

e. an oblique way of expressing wants or needs in order to save face for the recipient

f. a description of where the speaker stands on an issue, what he or she wants, or how he or she plans to act in the future

g. a process in which two or more parties discuss specific proposals in order to find a mutually acceptable agreement

h. a nonassertive response style in which the communicator submits to a situation rather than attempt to have his or her needs met

i. the inability to express one's thoughts or feelings when necessary

j. a relational conflict style in which the approach of the partners varies from one situation to another

k. an indirect expression of aggression, delivered in a way that allows the sender to maintain a façade of kindness

l. a relational conflict style in which partners use different but mutually reinforcing behaviors

m. an approach to conflict resolution in which one party reaches its goal at the expense of the other

Harcourt Brace & Company

_____ 19. win–lose problem solving

_____ 20. win–win problem solving

n. an expressed struggle between at least two interdependent parties who perceive incompatible goals, scarce rewards, and interference

o. an approach to conflict resolution in which the parties work together to satisfy all their goals

p. a pattern of managing disagreements that repeats itself over time in a relationship

q. an unacknowledged repeating pattern of interlocking behavior used by participants in a conflict

r. a relational conflict style in which both partners use the same tactics

s. an explanation of the results that follow from either the behavior of the person to whom the message is addressed or from the speaker's interpretation of the addressee's behavior

t. an approach to conflict resolution in which neither side achieves its goals

TRUE/FALSE

Mark the statements below as true or false. Correct statements that are false on the lines below to create a true statement.

_____ 1. A conflict can exist only when both parties are aware of a disagreement.

_____

_____

_____ 2. Conflict will occur only if there is not enough of something (money, love, respect, time, etc.) to go around.

_____

_____

_____ 3. Very close and compatible relationships will not involve conflict.

_____

_____

_____ 4. Effective communication during conflicts can actually keep good relationships strong.

_____

_____

_____ 5. Nonassertion is always a bad idea.

_____

_____

_____ 6. Verbally abusive couples report significantly less relational satisfaction than do partners who communicate about their conflicts in other ways.

_____

_____

_____ 7. Satisfied conflict partners tend to make more personal characteristic complaints than behavioral complaints.

_____

_____

_____ 8. Crazymaking is just another name for passive aggression.

_____

_____

_____ 9. "It takes two to tango"—in conflict, as in dancing, men and women behave in similar ways.

_____

_____

_____ 10. The most important cultural factor in shaping attitudes toward conflict is gender.

_____

_____

COMPLETION

Fill in the blanks with the crazymaker term described below.

avoiders   pseudoaccomodators   guiltmakers   subject changers   distracters
mind readers   trivial tyranizers   gunnysakers   beltliners   trappers

1. _____ don't respond immediately when they get angry. Instead, they let conflicts build up until they all pour out at once.

2. _____ do things they know will irritate their conflict partner rather than honestly sharing their resentments.

3. _____ engage in character analyses, explaining what the other person *really* means, instead of allowing their partners to express feelings honestly.

4. _____ set up a desired behavior for their partners and then when the behavior is met, they attack the very thing they requested.

5. _____ refuse to fight by leaving, falling asleep, or pretending to be busy.

6. _____ try to make their partners feel responsible for causing their pain even though they won't come right out and say what they feel or want.

7. _____ refuse to face up to a conflict either by giving in or by pretending that there's nothing at all wrong.

8. _____ use intimate knowledge of their partners to get them "where it hurts."

9. _____ attack other parts of their partner's life rather than express their feelings about the object of their dissatisfaction.

10. _____ escape facing up to aggression by shifting the conversation whenever it approaches an area of conflict.

MULTIPLE CHOICE

Identify which element of a clear message is being used in each statement according to the following key:

a. behavioral description
b. interpretation
c. feeling
d. consequence
e. intention

_____ 1. That's a good idea.

_____ 2. I'm worried about this course.

_____ 3. Jim looked angry today.

_____ 4. I want to talk to you about the $20 you borrowed.

_____ 5. I notice that you haven't been smiling much lately.

_____ 6. I don't know whether you're serious or not.

_____ 7. I'm glad you invited me.

_____ 8. Ever since then I've found myself avoiding you.

_____ 9. I'm sorry you didn't like my work.

_____ 10. I want you to know how important this is to me.

_____ 11. It looks to me like you meant to embarrass me.

_____ 12. After the party at Art's, you seemed to withdraw.

_____ 13. I see you're wearing my ring again.

_____ 14. From now on you can count on me.

_____ 15. I've never heard you say a curse word before.

_____ 16. . . . and since then I've been sleeping at my dad's house.

_____ 17. Because that occurred, they won't work overtime.

_____ 18. Dith sighed and looked out the window.

_____ 19. I'm excited about the possibility.

_____ 20. I'll get another place to live.

Choose the letter of the personal conflict style that is best illustrated by the behavior found below.

  a. avoidance
  b. accommodation
  c. direct aggression
  d. assertion
  e. indirect communication
  f. passive aggression

_____ 21. Stan keeps joking around to keep us from talking about commitment.

_____ 22. "I can't believe you were so stupid as to have erased the disk."

_____ 23. Even though he wanted to go to the party, Allen stayed home with Sara rather than hear her complain.

_____ 24. By mentioning how allergic she was to smoke, Joan hoped that her guest would smoke outside.

_____ 25. "When you smoke inside, I start to cough and my eyes water, so please go out on the balcony when you want to smoke."

_____ 26. Rather than tell Nick about his frustration over Nick's not meeting the deadline, Howard complained to others about Nick's unreliability while maintaining a smiling front to Nick.

_____ 27. Carol wouldn't answer the phone after their disagreement because she was afraid it would be Nancy on the other end.

Harcourt Brace & Company

_____ 28. Faced with his obvious distress, Nikki put her very important work aside to listen to him.

_____ 29. Even though Nikki could see Kham's distress, she told him she had a deadline to meet in one hour and asked if they could talk then.

_____ 30. (Sarcastically) "Oh, sure, I *loved* having dinner with your parents instead of going to the party Saturday night."

CHAPTER 10 STUDY GUIDE ANSWERS

MATCHING (KEY TERM REVIEW)

1.	h	5.	c	9.	b	13.	g	17.	p
2.	a	6.	n	10.	e	14.	i	18.	r
3.	d	7.	q	11.	f	15.	j	19.	m
4.	l	8.	s	12.	t	16.	k	20.	o

TRUE/FALSE

1.	T	3.	F	5.	F	7.	F	9.	F
2.	F	4.	T	6.	T	8.	T	10.	F

COMPLETION

1.	gunnysackers	5.	avoiders	9.	distractors
2.	trivial tyranizers	6.	guiltmakers	10.	subject changers
3.	mind readers	7.	pseudoaccomodators		
4.	trappers	8.	beltliners		

MULTIPLE CHOICE

1.	b	7.	c	13.	a	19.	c	25.	d
2.	c	8.	d	14.	e	20.	e	26.	f
3.	b	9.	c	15.	a	21.	a	27.	a
4.	e	10.	e	16.	d	22.	c	28.	b
5.	a	11.	b	17.	d	23.	b	29.	d
6.	b	12.	b	18.	a	24.	e	30.	f